S-974

Phi

Climbers
for walls and arbours

returned on or before

ROGER PHILLIPS
& MARTYN RIX

Research by Nicky Foy
Design Gill Stokoe, Jill Bryan & Debby Curry

A Pan Original

Acknowledgements

We would like to thank the following gardens and suppliers for allowing us to visit them and photograph their plants:
The Royal Botanic Garden, Edinburgh; the Royal Horticultural Society's Gardens at Wisley and Rosemoor; the Royal Botanic Gardens, Kew; the Royal National Rose Society's Gardens of the Rose; the Savill Garden, Windsor; La Mortola; Isola Bella; the Harry P. Leu Gardens, Florida; the Theodore Payne Foundation, Pasadena, California; Dumbarton Oaks, Washington DC; Cannington College; Tapeley Park; Castle Howard; Powis Castle; Chatsworth; Gravetye Manor; Eccleston Square gardens; Treasures of Tenbury; the Plantsman Nursery, Devon.
The following also helped us by allowing us to take photographs in their gardens, and in other ways:
William Waterfield, John Vanderplank, Guy and Emma Sisson; Sheila Bryan, Marilyn Inglis and Anne Thatcher.

First published 1998 by Pan
an imprint of Macmillan Publishers Limited
25 Eccleston Place, London SW1W 9NF
and Basingstoke
Associated companies throughout the world
ISBN 0-330-35549-X
Copyright in the text and illustrations
© Roger Phillips and Martyn Rix
The right of the authors to be identified as the authors of this work has been asserted by them in accordance with the Copyright, Designs and Patents Act 1988.
All rights reserved.

9 8 7 6 5 4 3 2 1
A CIP catalogue record for this book is available from the British Library

Colour Reproduction by Aylesbury Studios Ltd.
Printed by Butler and Tanner Ltd. Frome, Somerset

Contents

A Wiltshire cottage with climbing roses

Introduction

When planting or replanting a garden there are a great many things to be considered. Firstly, there is the structure of the planting from the trees down to the shrubs. Then there is the introduction of ground-cover, perennials and bulbs to add to the detail and flower colour. Last but by no means least, there is something that should never be forgotten, which is the planting of climbers.

Climbers are immensely useful plants in unifying a garden's layout which they achieve by scrambling across fences and shrubs, forming arches or covering fences and pergolas. Because they reach up towards the light, climbers like clematis are useful for planting in dark corners, while climbing roses add colour to trees, and honeysuckles and jasmines are wonderful for adding scent. In small town gardens, climbers are especially useful as they add an extra dimension to a small area by clothing the walls and fences with foliage and flowers and prolonging the season of interest of shrubs and trees. Plants with scented or aromatic leaves should be positioned near the paths or placed to grow over arbours, so that when you walk round the garden you will get the full impact of their aroma.

How to use this book

The two main groups of plants included in this book are those that can climb and support themselves by twining or scrambling up through trellises, shrubs and trees, and those that do well against walls or fences. Of the second group many, like cotoneasters, will need to be fixed to wires or a trellis, and others like sweet peas will need to be helped and guided to start climbing. For example, twigs pruned from deciduous trees and shrubs provide an effective early support at the same time as giving a natural look.

We have arranged the plants roughly in order of flowering, starting with spring and working through the seasons, based on the plants' normal flowering time in the cooler parts of the Northern Hemisphere. Within this framework, we have, where possible, grouped the plants more or less in families, selecting a few of the best from each group. The majority of plants are hardy but we have included a few tender plants as well which require greenhouse or other protection in northern Europe and eastern North America. They can, of course, be grown outside in warmer climates, such as Florida, California, the Mediterranean and Australia.

An approximate guide to hardiness is given for each plant in three ways; Fahrenheit, centigrade and the American Department of Agriculture hardiness zones. The natural world is flexible, so if you are prepared to try plants at the limits of their hardiness, you may be lucky (and pleasantly surprised). Always bear in mind that the drier the roots of a plant in winter, the hardier it is likely to be.

Clematis viticella 'Etiole Violette'

Solanum crispum 'Glasnevin'

Passiflora caerulea, with variegated ivy

A pillar of honeysuckle

Lonicera sempervirens

Choosing plants

Through the pages of this book, we aim to
provide inspiration for when you come to
choose your climbing plants. However, the
first thing to establish is which plants will do
well in your garden. Try looking at some of
the best gardens in your immediate area and
see which climbers are looking healthy and
flowering well. Have no fear of copying
someone else; all the best gardeners do it.
If you see a large-flowered white clematis
thriving, remember you can buy large-
flowered clematis in a range of colours with
especially good blues and purples, or you
may feel that you would like a small-flowered
yellow one. Use your neighbours' gardens as
a jumping-off point and try and build on the
plants that do well in your soil and weather
conditions.

Growing & siting plants

As with all plants, success in growing
climbing plants comes from providing
conditions as near as possible to their natural
habitat. Soil at the foot of walls tends to be
dry, so new plants are likely to need extra
water during their first summer, until they
become established. Make sure that the
roots are well soaked and water deeply and
seldom, so that the roots go deep and do not
stay on the surface. The only thing that
should be borne in mind specifically when
growing climbers is that they should have
sufficient room to grow to maturity.

Wisteria floribunda 'Alba' at Scotney Castle, Kent

A fine combination of climbers and wall shrubs at Powis Castle, with a variegated *Euonymus* in front

Where to obtain plants

Start by visiting your local nursery. There are numerous small nurseries which are a very good source of plants and they will know which plants thrive in your area. Where possible, choose young, actively growing plants, not those that have been sitting in their pots for months. Try to buy plants sold from the open ground or those grown in soil, as they will do better in an open garden than those grown in peat-based compost. Plants are grown in peat compost for the convenience of the grower, not the customer. If you have time, visit gardens open to the public, making notes of plants you like. You can then buy them locally or purchase them by mail order. Sources of the rarer plants can be found by looking in the following:

The RHS *Plant Finder*, devised by Chris Philip is published annually. It gives details of nurseries and the whole range of plants stocked in Britain. It is invaluable when searching for specific plants, but you will need to look under the Latin name (given in brackets next to the common name in this book). Obtainable in book shops. **The Andersen Horticultural Library's *Source List of Plants & Seeds*** is the American equivalent of *The Plant Finder*. Obtainable from A. H. L., Minnesota Landscape Arboretum, 3675 Arboretum Drive, P.O. Box 39, Chanhassen, MN 55317–0039, USA. ***PPP Index*** is the European *Plant Finder*, published both as a book and as a CD-ROM in German, French and English by Eugen Ulmer GmbH, Wollgrasweg 41, 70599 Stuttgart, Germany.

Hedera helix at Dumbarton Oaks

Ivy in an old chimney-pot

Ivy

Ivy is a small genus of 11 species of evergreen, woody, climbing or creeping plants. Ivies come from Europe, Asia and North Africa, but numerous variegated cultivars have been developed and are grown in gardens for their decorative effect. Because of its preference for shade, ivy makes an excellent ground-cover plant as well as being popular for growing up walls and buildings and as a houseplant.

PLANTING & PRUNING HELP

Hedera helix 'Goldheart'

Ivies thrive in shade and should never be placed in direct sunlight or allowed to dry out. They like a rich soil and in summer can be given a balanced liquid feed every two weeks to encourage vigorous growth. If being grown up a wall, they should be tied up until they become self-clinging. Ivies are easily propagated by cuttings which should be taken between June and October when the young growth has hardened sufficiently. Once well rooted they can be planted out or put into bigger pots to grow indoors.

A mixed group of ivies trained on a wall

Hedera helix and *Hedera helix* 'Glacier' at Harry P. Leu Gardens in Florida

Hedera helix A shrubby evergreen creeper or climber that grows to 100ft (30m) with clusters of greenish flowers in September and October, and black berries which ripen in spring. Hardy to −10°F (−23°C), US zones 6–9. Native to most of Europe except the far north. There are numerous cultivars of this plant of which a selection is listed below.

'Sagittifolia' This cultivar has very narrow green leaves.

'Glacier' Leaves are pale green in the centre with a narrow irregular white edge.

'Oro de Bogliasco' usually called **'Goldheart'**
The leaves are golden yellow in the centre and green at the edge.

Hedera helix 'Sagittifolia'

Hedera helix 'Sagittifolia'

IVIES

Hedera helix 'Cavendishii'

Hedera colchica

Hedera helix
'Cavendishii'

Hedera helix 'Buttercup' This climbing cultivar has leaves which are golden yellow, particularly at the top of the plant.

Hedera helix 'Cavendishii' This shrubby cultivar has leaves which are golden yellow around the edge, and berries which are reddish when young.

IVIES

Hedera colchica 'Dentata Variegata'

Hedera colchica   A large ivy, native to the north of Turkey, the south Caucasus and the Caspian coast of Iran. The stems grow to around 60ft (20m), the large leaves are almost unlobed. **'Sulphur Heart'**   The leaves are predominantly yellow in the centre with green edges and veining. **'Dentata Variegata'**   Green leaves with yellow edges that get paler and increase in size as the plant ages.

Hedera colchica 'Sulphur Heart'

Hedera helix 'Buttercup'

Camellia sasanqua 'Narumigata'

Camellia × *williamsii* 'Anticipation'

Camellia reticulata 'Nuccio's Ruby'

Camellias

Camellia is a genus of about 250 species of evergreen shrubs or trees. They come from Asia, specifically northern India and the Himalayas, east to Japan and northern Indonesia, but have been cultivated for centuries and are now grown as garden plants in numerous countries. In warm, temperate climates, camellias are grown on walls and as hedges and street trees as well as being used for topiary. Because they are tolerant of salt and pollution, they are useful shrubs for growing in seaside areas and large towns.

PLANTING HELP   Camellias thrive best in soil that is composed of slightly acid sand or light topsoil with plenty of organic matter in it. Most important of all is that it is well-drained, as water-logging of the plants is fatal. They need cool winters and many will tolerate mild frosts, but they need warmth and sunlight in late summer to form the flower buds that appear the following autumn, winter or spring. As camellias are long-lived, provide plenty of space for growth and prune in spring after flowering before the young growth starts. Camellias can also be grown successfully in a greenhouse, either in the ground or in pots. Once established all camellias benefit from the addition of some fertilizer but be careful not to over-fertilize.

Camellia reticulata 'Captain Rawes'
An evergreen shrub that grows to 12ft (3.5m) tall, with large, deep pink flowers in late winter and early spring. Hardy to 20°F (−6°C), US zones 9–10. This variety was the original introduction made by Robert Fortune from China in the early 19th century.

Camellia reticulata 'Nuccio's Ruby'
An evergreen shrub that grows to 12ft (3.5m) tall, with large, deep red, wavy-petalled, semi-double flowers that appear in spring. Hardy to 20°F (−6°C), US zones 9–10.

Camellia × williamsii 'Anticipation'
A rather erect, bushy evergreen shrub that grows to 16ft (4.5m) tall, with abundant, strong pink flowers that appear in spring. Hardy to 10°F (−12°C), US zones 8–10 or lower.

Camellia sasanqua 'Narumigata'
An evergreen shrub that grows to 16ft (4.5m) tall, with scented, creamy white flowers flecked with pink at the edges that appear in autumn. Hardy to 10°F (−12°C), US zones 8–10.

Camellia reticulata 'Captain Rawes' in the conservatory at Chatsworth

Camellia japonica 'Apollo' in Eccleston Square

Camellia japonica

Japonicas are the hardiest group of camellias, normally hardy down to 10°F (−12°C), US zones 8–10 or below; however the flowers are easily damaged by cold winds. In cold areas flowers will fare better and receive less damage if the plants are grown on a warm wall. They are normally rather slow-growing, reaching a height of about 6ft (2m) after 10 or 12 years; eventually, however, they will grow to the size of a small tree.

Camellia japonica '**C. M. Hovey**'   Has a robust, vigorous growth and free-flowering, dark crimson blooms.

Camellia japonica '**Bernice Boddy**'
Introduced in 1946, this variety has a vigorous upright growth and lovely white flowers tipped with pale pink.

Camellia japonica '**Christmas Beauty**'
This variety has deep pink flowers and a rather lax growth which needs support.

Camellia japonica '**Apollo**'   Confusingly, there are a number of plants with this name. This, the correct one, is free-flowering with a strong growth and red blooms.

Camellia japonica
'**Debutante**'
A slow-growing variety that has lovely, very pale, white pink flowers.

'Debutante'

CAMELLIAS

Camellia japonica 'Christmas Beauty'

Camellia japonica 'Tom Thumb'

Camellia japonica 'C. M. Hovey'

Camellia japonica 'Finlandia'

Camellia japonica 'Bernice Boddy'

Camellia japonica 'Finlandia'   Named in 1937, this variety has white flowers and medium growth.

Camellia japonica 'Tom Thumb'   Of medium, upright growth, this variety has sugar-pink flowers with a white edge to the petals.

Camellia japonica 'Yours Truly'   This variety has a medium bushy growth and pink flowers that become paler towards the edge of the petals, which are edged very pale pink to white.

Camellia japonica 'Yours Truly'

Exochorda × *macrantha* 'The Bride' in Eccleston Square

Exochorda

Exochorda × macrantha **'The Bride'**
A spreading deciduous shrub that grows to 5ft (1.5m) tall and more across, with creamy white flowers in early spring along arching branches. Hardy to 0°F (−18°C), US zones 7–10 or a little more.

PLANTING HELP   Thrives in any soil and likes sun or part shade and a warm position. It makes an excellent plant for the front of a shrubby border; in early spring the profuse flowering will be a delight.

Japanese Quince

Chaenomeles are very early-flowering shrubs with delicate waxy flowers. They are useful for any garden, especially when trained on a sunny wall. They have the additional value of producing fruits that resemble, in shape and taste, small quinces, and are much used in Chinese medicine, particularly for the treatment of cramp.

PLANTING HELP
Although *Chaenomeles* can be grown as shrubs, they are excellent when trained on sunny walls, allowing the flowers to be much more easily seen and more freely produced in cool climates. They grow well in most soils but will show some chlorosis in very limy soils.

*Chaenomeles
cathayensis*

Chaenomeles speciosa **'Moerloosei'**
A deciduous shrub that grows up to 7ft (2m) tall and wide, with small clusters of large creamy white to pinkish flowers in spring. Hardy to −20°F (−29°C), US zones 5–9.

*Chaenomeles ×
superba* **'Rowallane'**
A deciduous shrub that grows to 5ft (1.5m) tall and wide against a wall, but less in the open, with small clusters of scarlet flowers that appear in spring. Hardy to −20°F (−29°C), US zones 5–9.

Chaenomeles cathayensis
A deciduous shrub or small tree that grows to 10ft (3m) tall, with pink flowers in March and April. Hardy to 0°F (−18°C), US zones 7–10 or a little more. Native to China.

'Rowallane'

Exochorda × macrantha 'The Bride'

Chaenomeles speciosa 'Moerloosei'

Ceanothus 'Concha' at Cannington

Ceanothus

Ceanothus or California Lilac belongs to the family *Rhamnaceae* and is a genus about 60 species of woody deciduous or evergreen shrubs or small trees. Native to North America, predominantly the west, from SW Canada down to northern Mexico. All species in the genus can hybridize with each other, which has resulted in numerous hybrid-cultivars and a great deal of confusion with names. The evergreen varieties are valued for their glossy foliage and all are popular in gardens for their range of pretty blue to mauve flowers, either in mixed borders or free-standing. Most varieties are also well-suited to growing in coastal gardens.

PLANTING HELP   Ideally, soil should be light and freely draining, and while many species will tolerate some lime in the soil, shallow chalky soils are not favoured. Plant in a warm, sunny position with full sun or part-day shade and sheltered from cold, drying winds. Most will tolerate some degree of frost but plant in the shelter of a warm south-facing wall if there is danger of prolonged frost and freezing winds.

Ceanothus 'Concha'   An evergreen shrub that grows to 7ft (2m) tall, with long flower heads of lilac blue flowers that burst from red buds in late spring. Hardy to 10°F (–12°C), US zones 8–10.

Ceanothus cyaneus   A large, rapid-growing shrub that reaches 16ft (4.5m), with brilliant blue, scented flower heads that appear in early summer. Native to California. Hardy to 20°F (–6°C), US zones 9–10.

Ceanothus 'Cascade'   A cultivated form of *Ceanothus thyrsiflorus* with a lovely weeping habit; this evergreen shrub grows to 16ft (4.5m) tall, with good blue flowers that appear in late spring. Hardy to 10°F (–12°C), US zones 8–10.

Ceanothus dentatus **var.** *floribundus*
An evergreen shrub that grows to 7ft (2m) tall, with dark blue flowers in early summer. Native to California. Hardy to 20°F (–6°C), US zones 9–10.

Ceanothus 'Concha'

Ceanothus 'Cascade' in Eccleston Square with *Clematis montana*

Ceanothus dentatus var. *floribundus* with
Ceanothus 'Concha' behind

Ceanothus cyaneus

CEANOTHUS

Ceanothus 'Eleanor Taylor'

Ceanothus 'Delight'   An evergreen shrub that grows to 24ft (7m) tall, often with a short, stout trunk and lilac blue flower heads in late spring. Hardy to 10°F (−12°C), US zones 8–10.

Ceanothus 'Frosty Blue'

Ceanothus 'Eleanor Taylor'   An evergreen shrub that grows to 10ft (3m) tall and the same in width, with delicate pink buds which open into light blue flowers in spring. A little known American variety. Hardy to 10°F (−12°C), US zones 8–10.

Ceanothus 'Frosty Blue'   A somewhat tender variety with large clusters of blue flowers that have frosty white touches. They appear in late spring and summer. Hardy to 20°F (−6°C), US zones 9–10.

Ceanothus 'Puget Blue'   An evergreen shrub that grows to 17ft (5m) tall against a wall, with clusters of dense lilac flowers that appear in late spring. Hardy to 10°F (−12°C), US zones 8–10.

Ceanothus 'Southmead'
An evergreen shrub that grows to 10ft (3m) tall, with large flower heads of brilliant blue flowers that appear in spring. Hardy to 10°F (−12°C), US zones 8–10.

Ceanothus 'Southmead'

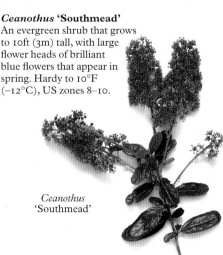

Ceanothus 'Southmead'

Ceanothus 'Puget Blue'

Ceanothus 'Delight' in Eccleston Square

Ceanothus 'Eleanor Taylor'

Acacia baileyana

Mimosa or Acacia

Mimosas (or Wattles, as they are usually known in their native Australia) are part of the large genus *Acacia*, containing over 900 species of trees and shrubs, native to the tropical and warm temperate areas of the world, especially Australia and Africa.

PLANTING HELP   Mimosas will normally grow in any reasonably well-drained, preferably moist and not very limy garden soil, although they will tolerate drought. They are not very hardy, although they can be grown outside in some northern climates with the protection of a south-facing wall. In cooler areas mimosas make some of the best winter-flowering shrubs for a tall conservatory or greenhouse.

Acacia baileyana   An evergreen shrub or small tree that grows to 33ft (10m) tall, with clusters of tiny, golden yellow flowers in late winter. Native to Australia but widely cultivated. Hardy to about 10°F (−12°C), US zones 8–10.

Acacia dealbata   An evergreen shrub or tree that grows to 33ft (10m) tall in colder climates but as much as 100ft (30m) in mild climates. It has clusters of tiny yellow, fragrant flowers in winter to early spring. Native to Australia and Tasmania, commonly grown in California and the south of France, and sold in florists in England in February. Hardy to about 20°F (−6°C), US zones 9–10.

Acacia pravissima   A bushy shrub or small tree that grows to 26ft (8m) tall, with bright yellow flowers in spring. Its unique feature is the holly-like foliage. Native to SE Australia. Found to be the most hardy of the Australian acacias, to about 10°F (−12°C), US zones 8–10.

Carpenteria

Carpenteria californica   A sprawling or upright evergreen shrub that grows to 12ft (3.5m) tall, with large white flowers in May to July. Native to California. Hardy to 10°F (−12°C), US zones 8–10 or a bit more.

Acacia dealbata in Lawrence Johnston's garden at Serre de la Madone in January

Fremontodendron in California

PLANTING HELP   This will grow best when it is planted against a south-facing wall where the added heat will encourage better flowering. Soil should be well-drained, and like many shrubs from California, it is very tolerant of drought.

Acacia pravissima

Cytisus

Cytisus battandieri   A rather spindly, semi-evergreen shrub that grows to 13ft (4m), with pineapple-scented, yellow flowers in June. Native to North Africa, around Morocco. Hardy to about 0°F (–18°C), US zones 7–10.

PLANTING HELP   Thrives in well-drained light soil and full sun. It looks most attractive when trained on a wall.

Fremontodendron

***Fremontodendron* 'California Glory'**
This hybrid is a fast-growing, showy but short-lived shrub or small tree, with large yellow flowers from spring to late summer. Hardy to about 10°F (–12°C), US zones 8–10 or a little less.

PLANTING HELP   Likes hot, dry, well-drained soil and full sun with wall protection.

Cytisus battandieri

'California Glory'

Carpenteria californica

Sophora microphylla in New Zealand

*Sophora
microphylla*

Sophora

Sophora microphylla A deciduous shrub or
small tree that grows to 17ft (5m) tall, with pinnate
leaves and bright yellow pea flowers in spring.
Native to New Zealand. Hardy to 10°F (−12°C),
US zones 8–10.

PLANTING HELP Thrives in full sun
and well-drained soil, with wall protection in
frosty areas.

Hardenbergia

Hardenbergia violacea   An evergreen climber with stems that grow to 7ft (2m), single leaflets and masses of small purple flowers in spring; native to Australia. Hardy to about 20°F (–6°C), US zones 9–10 or a little less.

PLANTING HELP   *Hardenbergia* thrives in any sandy soil in full sun or part shade. Keep dry in summer.

Buddleja

Hardenbergia violacea

A large genus of deciduous and evergreen shrubs from Asia, Africa and America. We illustrate some of the more tender species which benefit from the protection of a wall. They all have delicious and subtle scents.

PLANTING HELP   These *Buddlejas* thrive in any soil and full sun. Unless you live in a nearly frost-free area, they are best grown in a conservatory where they will be protected during their flowering period.

Buddleja colvilei   A very large deciduous shrub that grows to 24ft (7m) tall, with big drooping clusters of scented, pink or wine-red flowers in early summer. Native to the Himalayas. Hardy to 10°F (–12°C), US zones 8–10.

Buddleja officinalis   An evergreen shrub that grows to 8ft (2.5m) tall, with rounded clusters of scented, pale mauve flowers in early spring. Native to China. Hardy to about 20°F (–6°C), US zones 9–10 or a little less.

Buddleja colvilei outdoors at Tapeley Park

Buddleja crispa

A deciduous shrub that grows to 13ft (4m) or more, with fragrant, sugar-pink flowers that appear in spring if not pruned, but in summer to autumn if pruned in spring. Native to the Himalayas and China. Hardy to about 10°F (–12°C), US zones 8–10 or a little less.

Buddleja crispa

Buddleja officinalis flowering on a wall in Kent

25

Wisteria sinensis at Rosemoor, Devon

Wisteria floribunda

Wisteria floribunda 'Rosea'

Wisteria

Wisteria belongs to the pea and bean family and is a small genus of about 10 species of deciduous, twining, woody vines in which the older stems become gnarled, fissured trunks. Wisterias are grown over arches, trellises, up walls and around porches for their pretty foliage and lovely, pendulous clusters of flowers that range from white to blue, mauve and pink and are generally scented. They are native to China, Japan and eastern North America, and numerous hybrids and cultivars have been developed over the centuries in China and Japan and, more recently, in Europe and America.

Wisteria sinensis

PLANTING & PRUNING HELP Wisterias should be planted in deep, fertile soil that is well-drained but water-retentive. They will flourish best in a sunny or southwest facing position with some protection from early morning frost or wind. The objective of pruning wisteria is to encourage flowering spurs to grow out from the wall. Pruning of the summer shoots at the end of August will encourage the production of more flower buds and then further pruning should be done in the winter to remove the long trailing shoots that may have grown at the back of the wall.

Wisteria floribunda A woody climbing and twining deciduous shrub that grows to 70ft (20m). The violet blue scented flowers hang down in racemes up to 3½ft (1m) long and bloom in early summer. They flourish in any soil, in full sun but require heat from a wall in cooler climates. Hardy to 0°F (−18°C), US zones 7–10. Native to Japan.

***Wisteria floribunda* 'Rosea'** A pale pinkish form with racemes to 18in (45cm) long.

***Wisteria floribunda* 'Alba'** In this form the flowers are white or very pale mauve with racemes 10–16in (25–40cm) long.

Wisteria sinensis A woody climbing and twining deciduous shrub that grows to 130ft (40m). The bluish lilac flowers hang in racemes up to 12in (30cm) long and bloom in early summer, often producing a second, poorer crop two months later. It flourishes in any soil in full sun or part shade. Hardy to 10°F (−12°C), US zones 8–10. Native to China.

Wisteria × formosa A hybrid between *Wisteria floribunda* and *W. sinensis* in which all the flowers of a raceme open together. It grows to 132ft (40m). Hardy to 0°F (−18°C), US zones 7–10.

Wisteria × formosa

Wisteria floribunda 'Alba'

Jasminum polyanthum climbing along a wall around a beautiful old jar in a garden in Madeira

Jasmine

Jasmine belongs to the Olive family *Oleaceae*, and is a very large genus of about 200 evergreen or deciduous shrubs or woody climbers. They come from the tropical and temperate regions of the Old World, with one species from America. There are also numerous cultivars. Jasmines are grown principally for their wonderful, deeply fragrant flowers, and should be trained up pergolas, arches, walls and fences or supported on trelliswork. They also make excellent conservatory plants.

PLANTING & PRUNING HELP   Plant jasmines in well-drained but moisture-retentive soil, where possible in a sheltered, sunny site. Frost-tender species do well in pots in a cool greenhouse or conservatory in fertile, loam-based soil with wires for support. Water regularly in summer, sparingly in winter and make sure they are well ventilated. Most species do not require much pruning but overgrown plants should be thinned as needed after flowering.

Jasminum officinale   A woody deciduous climber that grows to 13ft (4m) and sometimes considerably more, with highly fragrant white flowers that bloom in late summer. Hardy to 0°F (–18°C), US zones 7–10. Native to the Middle East, Himalayas and China. The form *affine*, sometimes called 'Grandiflorum' has the best flowers, tinged pink outside.

Jasminum officinale

Jasminum humile An evergreen or semi-evergreen deciduous shrub that grows to 7ft (2m) or more, with clusters of mildly fragrant yellow flowers that bloom during the summer. Hardy to 10°F (−12°C), US zones 8–10. Native to the Middle East, Himalayas and China.

Jasminum polyanthum A climbing shrub that grows to 24ft (7m) with masses of white, scented flowers that develop from crimson buds. Easily grown in good soil but it needs full sun to flower well. Rather tender, possibly hardy to 20°F (−6°C), US zones 9–10, with some protection.

Jasminum beesianum
A woody deciduous climber that grows to 10ft (3m). The small flowers can vary from pale to dark pink. Hardy to 10°F (−12°C), US zones 8–10.

Pandorea jasminoides
Bower Plant A twining evergreen shrub that grows to 17ft (5m). Best grown in a conservatory, it will look terrific if it is allowed to grow to the ceiling and then tumble down. There are white and pink varieties. Hardy to 32°F (0°C), US zone 10.

Trachelospermum jasminoides A twining evergreen shrub that grows to 24ft (7m) with clusters of highly fragrant white flowers that bloom from mid- to late summer. Hardy to 20°F (−6°C), US zones 9–10. In cold areas it may be planted in a pot and brought indoors on frosty nights. Native to China and Taiwan.

Trachelospermum jasminoides

Jasminum beesianum

Pandorea jasminoides 'Lady Di'

Jasminum humile with a white rose

Clematis

Clematis belongs to the Buttercup family, and is a large genus of about 200 species of deciduous or evergreen climbers or perennials. They come mainly from the Northern Hemisphere, although there are some notable species in New Zealand.

PLANTING & PRUNING HELP

Almost all clematis have a climbing habit and the leaf stalks will twist around anything they come in contact with. If growing against a bare wall, it will be necessary to provide some support, such as vertical wires, coarse netting or another plant, otherwise the clematis will trail at ground level and get into a knotty tangle. Although clematis climbs relentlessly upwards in search of light, the roots in the wild are in shade. Cultivated varieties also

Clematis armandii

prefer to have their roots in a shady spot, which can, perhaps, be created by growing another plant or putting small slabs near the base of the plant to protect the root system.

Clematis are best planted in spring or autumn and will grow in either acid or alkaline soils and even heavy clay soils as long as they are rich in nutrients and care is taken to create good drainage. Plenty of watering is essential from first planting until well established, and also during prolonged dry weather. Pruning is very important in the care of clematis and all newly planted specimens, especially those in containers, need to be pruned hard the first spring after planting so that they become bushy and strong at the base.

Clematis are generally pest-free but clematis wilt can be a problem for young plants, especially of the large-flowered varieties. If the plant wilts, all top growth should be removed and burnt and the plant cut back to soil level. If it has been planted deep enough, it should grow back. As many of the plants available are now much stronger, this is not such a problem as it was in the past. Preventive drenching with a systemic fungicide from spring until late summer should keep clematis wilt at bay in areas where it has occurred before.

Clematis × durandii A deciduous scrambling shrub or low climber that that grows to 8ft (2.5m) with deep violet blue flowers up to 4¼in (11cm) across in late summer. The leaves are glossy green and up to 5in (12cm) long. It will grow in any soil in sun or part shade and it is best grown through other plants for support. Prune hard in spring.

Clematis cirrhosa

Clematis × durandii growing on a low wall

Hardy to 20°F (−6°C), US zones 9–10. A hybrid between *C.* × *jackmannii* and *C. integrifolia* raised in 1870.

Clematis armandii   An evergreen climber that grows to 17ft (5m) with scented white or pink flowers 1¼–2½in (3–6cm) across in April or May. It will grow in any soil in sun or part shade with shelter. Hardy to 10°F (−12°C), US zones 8–10. Native to central and western China.

Clematis cirrhosa   An evergreen climber that grows to 17ft (5m) with scented cream flowers, occasionally spotted red, up to 2¾in (7cm) across from November to April. The silky tassels of the fruiting heads, produced in May, are more conspicuous than the flowers. Easily grown on a warm wall or in a sunny, sheltered position up a tree. Hardy to 10°F (−12°C), US zones 8–10. Native to the Mediterranean region.

Clematis macropetala   A deciduous climbing shrub that grows to 10ft (3m) with mauvish blue flowers up to 2in (5cm) across in early summer. It flourishes in any soil, sun or part shade and needs no pruning. Hardy to −10°F (−23°C), US zones 6–9. Native to Siberia and N China.

Clematis rehderiana   A deciduous climber that grows to 25ft (8m) with scented pale yellow nodding flowers up to ½in (1.5cm) long from June to September. The pinnate leaves are up to 9in (23cm) long with 7–9 leaflets. It will grow in any soil in full sun. Hardy to 0°F (−18°C), US zones 7–10. Native to W China.

Clematis tangutica var. obtusiuscula
A robust climber that grows to 10ft (3m) with rich yellow flowers up to 2½in (6cm) across from June to September. The green pinnate leaves are slightly toothed. Hardy to 0°F (−18°C), US zones 7–10. Native to China.

Clematis tangutica var. *obtusiuscula*

Clematis rehderiana at Kew

Clematis macropetala 'Maidwell Hall'

Clematis montana f. *grandiflora* at Sissinghurst

Clematis alpina 'Ruby'

Spring-flowering Clematis

There are so many varieties of clematis that it is possible to find them flowering at almost any time of year in either the garden or conservatory. The varieties of *C. montana* are some of the best for climbing up or over buildings, walls, trees and large shrubs; the smaller *C. alpina* can be grown in herbaceous borders or pots.

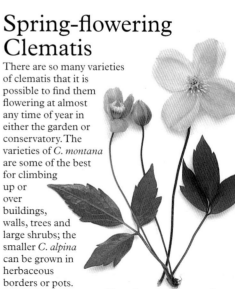

Clematis montana var. *rubens*

CLEMATIS

Clematis alpina 'Grandiflora'
A deciduous climber that grows to 8ft (2.5m) with large bluish or rarely pure white flowers, 2–3in (5–8cm) across in late spring. The fresh, light green leaves are serrated. It will grow in any well-drained soil in partial shade or with shaded roots. Hardy to −10°F (−23°C), US zones 6–9. Native to Europe and N Asia.

Clematis alpina 'Grandiflora'

Clematis alpina 'Ruby' A deciduous climber that grows to 8ft (2.5m) with soft red flowers, 2–3in (5–8cm) across in late spring. The fresh, light green leaves are sharply toothed. It will grow in any well-drained soil in partial shade or with shaded roots. Hardy to −20°F (−29°C), US zones 5–9. Native to Europe and N Asia.

Clematis montana A deciduous climber that grows to 20ft (6m) or more with white flowers 2–3in (5–8cm) across in late spring. The leaves

have three leaflets and are 2¾in (7cm) long. It will grow in any soil, preferably with a northern aspect, and it requires no pruning. Forma *grandiflora* has particularly large white flowers. Hardy to 10°F (−12°C), US zones 8–10. Native to the Himalayas and western China.

Clematis montana 'Elizabeth' A deciduous climber with a slight vanilla fragrance that grows to 20ft (6m) or more with pale pink flowers 2–3in (5–8cm) across, that bloom in late spring.

Clematis montana var. rubens A deciduous climber that grows to 20ft (6m) or more with pink or white, pink-backed flowers 2–3in (5–8cm) across, in early summer. The leaves are coloured purplish to bronze. Introduced to Europe from China in 1900.

Clematis montana 'Tetrarose' A deciduous climber that grows to 20ft (6m) or more with large, thick-textured deep pink flowers up to 4in (10cm) across in late spring. The leaves are bronze, up to 3in (8cm) long and the stems are tinted dark red. A very robust variety, a tetraploid, raised in Holland.

Clematis montana 'Tetrarose'

Clematis montana over a double red Hawthorn

Clematis montana 'Elizabeth'

Clematis viticella 'Kermesina'

Clematis viticella
'Margot Koster'

Clematis viticella

This group of very healthy and vigorous climbers is wonderful growing up small trees or through shrubs. The medium-sized flowers appear from summer into early winter, and the plants, being Mediterranean in origin, thrive in warm summer climates and sandy soils.

Clematis viticella **'Abundance'** A vigorous, very free-flowering deciduous climber that grows to 7ft (2m) with rose red flowers up to 2in (5cm) across which appear from midsummer to early autumn. Hardy to 10°F (−12°C), US zones 8–10.

Clematis viticella **'Alba Luxurians'**
A woody climber that grows from 8–20ft (2.5–6m) with white flowers up to 3in (8cm) across that appear from midsummer to early autumn. The first flowers of this vigorous cultivar are often completely green but the later ones are white, sometimes with green tips to the sepals.

Clematis **'Gravetye Beauty'** A vigorous sub-shrubby climber that grows to around 6ft (2m) and has crimson flowers up to 3in (8cm) across which bloom in summer. Rather short-lived in Britain, it likes a warm sunny or semi-shady position and needs to be pruned hard. Hardy to −20°F (−29 °C), US zones 5–9. A hybrid of *Clematis texensis*.

Clematis
'Gravetye
Beauty'

Clematis viticella **'Kermesina'** (syn. *Clematis viticella* 'Rubra') A very vigorous hybrid that grows to 20ft (6m) with free-flowering, wine-red flowers that open from mid- to late summer. It requires hard pruning.

Clematis viticella
'Margot Koster'
A vigorous woody climber that grows to 8ft (2.5m) with abundant, deep lilac pink flowers up to 4in (10cm) across that appear in late summer. After flowering it requires hard pruning.

Clematis viticella
'Purpurea Plena Elegans'
A vigorous climber that grows up to 10ft (3m) with very double, deep violet flowers up to 3in (8cm) across that appear from midsummer to early autumn. After flowering it requires hard pruning.

Clematis viticella
'Purpurea Plena
Elegans'

Clematis viticella 'Alba Luxurians'

Clematis viticella 'Abundance'

Large-flowered Clematis

There are about 300 named cultivars of clematis. The large-flowered clematis appeared when Chinese cultivars were introduced to the West in the mid-19th century; breeders soon crossed them with European species to create numerous cultivars, many of which are still popular today. Large-flowered hybrids, which come in a great variety of shades from crimson to lavender blue and white with a few yellow species, are spectacular plants that can be used in many ways. They can be planted to flop over ground-cover plants or grown through bushes or trained up poles, trellises, tennis-court netting and walls. The large-flowered clematis cultivars basically fall into two categories: those that flower early on the previous season's stems; and those that flower on the current season's stems from June onwards. The second group is more inclined to be susceptible to clematis wilt (*see page 30*). All are hardy to 0°F (–18°C), US zones 7–10.

Clematis 'Elsa Späth'

Clematis 'Dr Ruppel'   This woody climber can grow up to 12ft (3.5m) or more and has rose-coloured flowers with a darker midstripe that bloom in summer and early autumn. It does not require any pruning.

Clematis 'Elsa Späth' (syns. 'Xerxes' and 'Blue Boy')   A woody climber that grows 7–10ft (2–3m) tall with large, deep purple flowers with a darker stripe down the middle, produced in spring and then again in autumn.

Clematis florida 'Alba Plena' (syn. *Clematis florida* 'Plena')   Commonly cultivated in the 19th century, but now rather rare, this old Japanese garden variety grows 7–10ft (2–3m) with white flowers. It flourishes best in a sunny position and needs to be pruned hard.

Clematis × jackmanii   A deciduous climber that grows to 12ft (3.5m) with large, violet purple flowers up to 5in (12cm) across which bloom from summer to autumn. This famous hybrid, raised in Woking in 1860, does well in any situation but requires hard pruning.

Clematis 'Nelly Moser'   This very popular hybrid grows to 12ft (3.5m) and has large, pink-striped flowers up to 7in (18cm) across that appear profusely in early summer and then again in late summer. Plant in a shady position to avoid the colour bleaching and prune lightly.

Clematis 'Perle d'Azur'   A vigorous *jackmanii* hybrid that grows to 15ft (4.5m) with sky blue to blue mauve flowers up to 6in (15cm) across that bloom profusely in mid- to late summer. Happy in sun or semi-shade, it only needs light pruning.

Clematis 'Sylvia Denny'   A woody climber with double white flowers up to 4in (10cm) across in early summer. Flourishes best in sun or semi-shade and only needs light pruning.

Clematis × jackmanii

Clematis 'Perle d'Azur'

Clematis 'Nelly Moser' on the pillar of an old shed

Clematis florida 'Alba Plena'

Clematis 'Dr Ruppel'

Clematis 'Sylvia Denny'

LARGE-FLOWERED CLEMATIS

A large-flowered clematis, possibly 'Gipsy Queen', on an old wall at Castle Howard

Clematis **'Beauty of Richmond'** A vigorous cultivar with large pink mauve flowers with a greenish midstripe, up to 6in (15cm) across that bloom from midsummer onwards. It will thrive in any situation and only requires light pruning.

Clematis **'Beauty of Worcester'** A less vigorous grower than some others, this cultivar produces cerise purple double flowers on old wood from early midsummer, and single flowers on young wood until early autumn. It prefers a sunny position and only requires light pruning.

Clematis **'Belle of Woking'** A not particularly vigorous old hybrid that has large, very pale pink double flowers up to 6in (15cm) across in late spring. It prefers a sunny position and only requires light pruning.

Clematis **'Jackmanii Rubra'** An old, fairly vigorous climber with dark red, semi-double flowers during midsummer, followed by single flowers until early autumn. It only requires light pruning.

Clematis **'Lord Nevill'** A vigorous cultivar that grows to about 20ft (6m) with large, dark violet blue to cerise flowers up to 7in (18cm) across which bloom from midsummer to early autumn. It only requires light pruning.

Clematis **'Gipsy Queen'** A vigorous climber with dark purple, velvety flowers to 5in (12cm) across in late summer and early autumn. It needs hard pruning.

Clematis **'Mrs Spencer Castle'** A moderately vigorous climber that grows to 17ft (5m) with large, pink double flowers in early summer and followed by single blooms in autumn. It only requires light pruning.

Clematis **'Proteus'** A moderately vigorous old hybrid with pink double flowers during the early summer and a second crop of single flowers in late summer. Thrives best away from full sun or deep shade and only requires light pruning.

Clematis **'The President'** A vigorous cultivar that grows to 12ft (3.5m) with large, slightly cup-shaped cerise purple flowers up to 7in (18cm) across produced freely in midsummer to early autumn. It only requires light pruning.

Clematis **'Vyvyan Pennell'** A vigorous hybrid that grows to 12ft (3.5m) with large, cerise purple double flowers up to 8in (20cm) produced in late spring or early summer and single, paler blooms produced on young wood in the autumn. It does not thrive in deep shade and only requires light pruning.

'Lord Nevill'

'Mrs Spencer Castle'

'Beauty of Richmond'

'Jackmanii Rubra'

'Beauty of Worcester'

'The President'

'Belle of Woking'

'Proteus'

'Vyvyan Pennell'

Specimens from Treasures of Tenbury, ¼ life-size

Honeysuckle

Lonicera × *americana*

for ground-cover, while the twining and climbing species are lovely grown up trellises, walls, pergolas, arches and fences.

PLANTING & PRUNING HELP
Honeysuckles will grow in sun or part shade with the bushy species flowering more profusely in a sunny situation. The climbers thrive best if the roots are in shade and the stems reach up to the sun. Evergreen climbers should be planted in the spring in rich, moist, well-drained soil, while the deciduous species should be planted in their dormant season. To establish a good framework and encourage branching, prune young specimens by shortening stems and then prune regularly to control growth and thin out old wood to prevent too much crowding after flowering.

Lonicera × *americana* A twiggy scrambling shrub that grows to 30ft (10m) with pink flowers that bloom in late spring through to early autumn. Hardy to 0°F (−18°C), US zones 7–10.

Honeysuckle or *Lonicera*, is a large genus containing about 180 species of bushy shrubs, with a few evergreen or deciduous twining climbers. They are very popular, diverse and long-lived plants which are grown for their lovely, often sweetly scented flowers. The bushy, shrubby varieties are excellent for mixed borders or even as hedging. Smaller, low-growing species can be used

Lonicera × *purpusii* A hybrid of *Lonicera standishii* and *Lonicera fragantissima* that grows to 10ft (3m). Hardy to −10°F (−23°C), US zones 6–9.

Lonicera periclymenum **'Belgica'** An early flowering form with the flowers are pink on the outside and cream within. Very fragrant in the evening. Hardy to −30°F (−35°C), US zones 4–8.

Lonicera periclymenum 'Graham Thomas' on a wall at the Savill Garden, Windsor

HONEYSUCKLE

Lonicera × brownii 'Fuchsioides'

Lonicera periclymenum 'Belgica'

Lonicera periclymenum 'Belgica'

Lonicera periclymenum 'Graham Thomas'
A deciduous climbing shrub to 13ft (4m), very
free-flowering, with cream flowers in summer and
autumn, which are very fragrant in the evening.
Hardy to 0°F (−18°C), US zones 7–10.

Lonicera × brownii 'Fuchsioides'   A twining
deciduous shrub that grows to 7ft (2m) with
terminal clusters of bright
orange-red flowers from late
spring to early autumn. Often
attacked by aphids, causing the
flowers to abort. Hardy to 10°F
(−12°C), US zones 8–10.

Lonicera standishii   A deciduous shrub that
grows to 8ft (2.5m) with sweetly scented, creamy
yellow flowers that appear in winter. Easily grown
but needs a warm summer or a place against a wall
to set a good crop of flower buds. Hardy to 10°F
(−12°C), US zones 8–10.

Lonicera standishii

Lonicera × purpusii

Lonicera tragophylla

Lonicera hildebrandiana A very large evergreen twining shrub that grows to 24ft (7m) with big heads of creamy white flowers that change to orange yellow, produced in the summer. Hardy to 32°F (0°C), US zones 10, or a little colder if given some protection.

Lonicera sempervirens Scarlet Trumpet Honeysuckle A vigorous twining evergreen shrub that grows 7–16ft (2–4.5m) with unscented orange red flowers in summer. Native to eastern

North America from Connecticut southwards. Hardy to –30°F (–35°C), US zones 4–8.

Lonicera similis A semi-evergreen twining shrub that grows 7–16ft (2–4.5m) with creamy flowers that are produced in summer to autumn. Similar to *Lonicera japonica*, but larger. Hardy to 20°F (–6°C), US zones 9–10.

Lonicera tragophylla A large deciduous twining shrub that grows to 20ft (6m) with big

HONEYSUCKLE

Lonicera hildebrandiana

Lonicera sempervirens

Lonicera × brownii 'Dropmore Scarlet'

Lonicera similis

clusters of yellow flowers that bloom in summer. It will flourish in any soil if there is shade at the root. Hardy to 0°F (–18°C), US zones 7–10.

***Lonicera × brownii* 'Dropmore Scarlet'**
A deciduous shrub that grows to 12ft (3.5m) with abundant bright scarlet flowers in summer. Hardy to –30°F (–35°C), US zones 4–8. Slightly scented.

Cape Honeysuckle *Tecomaria capensis* var. *lutea*
A low-growing sprawling shrub, native to South Africa, growing to 5ft (1.5m) with orange or yellow flowers through the summer. No relation to the true honeysuckle and unfortunately not scented. Hardy to 20°F (–6°C), US zones 9–10. It can be clipped to form a hedge.

Tecomaria capensis var. *lutea*

Mixed sweet peas on a trellis

Lathyrus odoratus 'Antique Fantasy Mixed'

Sweet Peas

Sweet peas belong to genus *Lathyrus* which contains about 110 species of annual or perennial herbs, frequently climbing by means of tendrils on the leaves. They come from Eurasia, North America, the mountains of East Africa and temperate South America.

The original scented sweet pea is native to Crete, Italy and Sicily. Many different cultivars of sweet pea have been developed and are valuable for cutting as well as for garden decoration. The other different wild species, shown on the next two pages, have lately become more frequently grown in gardens.

PLANTING HELP Sweet peas will thrive in any fairly fertile, well-drained soil in sun or part shade. If the soil is poor, a feed of general fertilizer and moisture-retentive compost is recommended before planting. Dead-head the plants throughout the flowering season. Seed may be sown either in

Sweet peas at Oran Park in New South Wales

the open or under glass in autumn, and wintered outside in a frost-free position, or in the open in spring in cold climates. Beware of mice, which can clear a planting of seeds in a couple of nights. It is worth remembering that most sweet peas are deliciously scented and therefore are best planted near a path or lawn.

Lathyrus odoratus In the wild form the flowers are purple or pink and appear in spring and summer. Hardy to −10°F (−23°C), US zones 6–10. There are numerous cultivars, some of which are listed below. The seeds are poisonous.

Lathyrus odoratus 'Jet Set'

'Antique Fantasy Mixed' This mixture of the older sweet-scented colour forms of the early sweet peas vary in colour from pure white to dark blackish purple. The flowers are slightly smaller than some of the most recent varieties.

'Blue Ice' This variety has lovely delicate blue mauve flowers.

'Jet Set' This is the name given to a group of sweet peas with a great variety of colours and very good scent. Bred in America.

Lathyrus odoratus 'Blue Ice' with others

Lathyrus splendens in Pasadena, California

Everlasting Peas

These species of *Lathyrus* generally have smaller flowers than the sweet peas, and are not scented. They are, however, useful perennial climbers for any garden. *Lathyrus latifolius*, in particular, is very valuable for its late flowering, and its tolerance of drought and poor soils. Dead-head religiously to prolong flowering.

PLANTING HELP   Perennial peas are most useful plants for scrambling over a fence or growing where they can scramble down a bank. They use tendrils to cling to pea sticks or living shrubs and do best in sunny positions in well-drained soil.

Lathyrus latifolius Everlasting Pea   A climbing or scrambling perennial that grows to 10ft (3m) with purplish pink or shell-pink flowers in loose clusters in summer. Hardy to 20°F (−29°C), US zones 5–9. Native to central and southern Europe and naturalized in Britain and North America.

***Lathyrus latifolius* 'White Pearl'**   The white form of *Lathyrus latifolius* can be raised with difficulty from cuttings or more easily from seed, in any soil in a warm position. A beautiful plant that will flower throughout the summer.

Lathyrus splendens   A lovely red perennial pea, native to California, where it is now very rare. A climber to 10ft (3m), flowering in spring. Hardy to 10°F (−12°C), US zones 8–10. It is to be hoped that this lovely species will soon be more widely grown and so its survival may become less uncertain.

Lathyrus grandiflorus   A suckering perennial, climbing to 5ft (1.5m), with pairs of round leaflets and solitary or paired, bright pink flowers around 1in (2.5cm) across. Hardy to 20°(−29°C), US zones 5–9. Native to southern Europe and North Africa. Beautiful but invasive in a border.

Lathyrus latifolius 'White Pearl'

Lathyrus latifolius

Lathyrus grandiflorus at Gravetye Manor, Sussex

Abutilon

Abutilon belongs to the Mallow family and is a large genus of about 150 species of perennial and annual herbs, shrubs and small trees. They come from the tropics and subtropics of the Americas, Africa, Asia and Australia. There are numerous hybrids of

Abutilon vitifolium

every hue, some with variegated foliage. There are varieties that are good for walls as well as summer bedding, for training on standards, for hanging baskets and growing in pots in conservatories.

PLANTING & PRUNING HELP   Abutilons will flourish in full sun or partial shade and prefer fertile, well-drained soil with sufficient water in dry spells. The first three abutilons listed here should be pruned in late winter just as the new growth is beginning. Most are hardy to 32°F (0°C), US zone 10 or a little less, for short periods in dry soil, and will do well in warm gardens. The last two are hardy to about 20°F (–6°C), US zones 9–10, if they are protected from freezing wind by a wall. In hot summer climates they need partial shade, ample humidity and water in dry places and are best suited to coastal climates in northern California and western Europe.

Abutilon × hybridum   A group of hybrids, most of which are upright shrubs with soft stems that grow to 10ft (3m) or more if supported. They have bell-shaped flowers with incurved petals in colours ranging from darkest red and pink, to yellow and white.
***Abutilon* 'Cerise Queen'**   This variety has rich pink flowers with spiralling overlapping petals.
***Abutilon* 'Moonchimes'**   This small plant has large, yellow, open bell-shaped or sometimes almost flat flowers.
***Abutilon* 'Silver Belle'**   This variety has white flowers with wide-spreading petals and dark yellow stamens.

Abutilon vitifolium   A fast-growing small shrub or tree that can grow to 33ft (10m) with pale violet flowers that bloom in spring and early summer. Prune after flowering. Native to southern Chile.
***Abutilon* 'Tennant's White'**   This is a white variety of the above.
***Abutilon* 'Veronica Tennant'**   This is a large pale-flowered selection.

Abutilon 'Tennant's White'

Abutilon 'Moonchimes'

Abutilon 'Silver Belle'

Abutilon 'Cerise Queen'

Abutilon 'Veronica Tennant' enjoying a sheltered position among other shrubs

Hibiscus 'Tylene'

Hibiscus 'Lady Bird'

Hibiscus 'Cooperi'

Hibiscus rosa-sinensis

Hibiscus 'All Aglow'

Hibiscus

Hibiscus belongs to the Mallow family and is a very large genus of about 220 species of annual or perennial herbs, shrubs, sub-shrubs and trees. They come from warm temperate, subtropical and tropical regions of the world, and numerous cultivars have also been developed.

PLANTING & PRUNING HELP

The cultivars of *Hibiscus rosa-sinensis* shown here require good drainage, protection from frosts and draughts and plenty of warmth and sun if they are to flower satisfactorily. They can be grown in conservatories in which the temperature does not fall lower than 32°F (0°C), US zone 10 or a little below, and do well outside in S California and Florida. Do not worry if many of the leaves fall off in winter as the plants will regenerate in the spring. Also, remember that the flowers of most cultivars only last for one day.

Hibiscus rosa-sinensis An evergreen shrub or tree that grows to about 17ft (5m) in the tropics and about 7ft (2m) in cultivation. The solitary

Hibiscus rosa-sinensis in the 17th-century garden on Isola Bella, Lake Maggiore

showy flowers have large petals and are generally red or deep red, darker towards the base. It is thought to be native to tropical Asia. Numerous forms have been developed since the mid-18th century. Hardy to 20°F (–6°C), US zones 9–10, if given a little protection.

Hibiscus 'All Aglow' A spectacular, tall single variety with very large orange flowers edged with red orange, centred with pink and white, and with a blotch of yellow on each petal. The petals overlap and are slightly ruffled.

Hibiscus 'Butterfly' This variety has single, bright yellow flowers.

Hibiscus 'Cooperi' A variety noted for its variegated narrow leaves splashed with pink and white. Large, bright red flowers are borne on a small bushy shrub.

Hibiscus 'Lady Bird' An upright bush of average height bearing large, single red blooms with prominent white or yellow veins and edge.

Hibiscus 'Tylene' A prolific, modern, upright-growing hybrid with large single flowers, mainly hyacinth blue, zoned and veined with white and with a small pink eye.

Hibiscus 'White Wings' This variety has large white flowers with a red throat.

Hibiscus 'White Wings'

Hibiscus 'Butterfly'

Schisandra glaucescens

Schisandra rubriflora

Specimens from Kew and Wisley, ¼ life-size

Akebia × pentaphylla

Akebia

Akebia quinata A vigorous evergreen climber that can grow up to 30ft (9m) tall and more in spread. The vanilla-scented, dark reddish purple brown flowers are male and female in the same cluster, with the male flowers at the apex being paler; they appear in late spring and early summer, sometimes followed by large, fleshy fruit. Hardy to −20°F (−29°C), US zones 5–9. Native to China, Korea and Japan.

Akebia × pentaphylla A hybrid between *Akebia quinata* and *Akebia trifoliata*, found wild in Japan and often cultivated.

PLANTING HELP These need a moisture-retentive, well-drained soil and are happy in full sun or partial shade. They are very fast growing and likely to become a nuisance in a small area.

Schisandra rubriflora with berries at Wisley

Akebia quinata

Schisandra rubriflora flowering well on the wall behind the Alpine House at Kew

Schisandra

A genus of about 25 deciduous and evergreen twining shrubs, native mainly in E Asia with one or two species in NE America. They are grown principally for their colourful strings of red berries, and a large plant in full fruit is a fine sight.

PLANTING HELP   Plant in any soil in sun or shade. As male and female flowers are on separate plants, they should be planted near each other to ensure a good crop of fruit. They need a moisture-retentive, well-drained soil. If grown on a wall they will need vertical wires to twine up.

Schisandra rubriflora (syn. *S. grandiflora* var. *rubriflora*)   A deciduous twining climber that grows to 25ft (8m) or more, with dull red flowers in spring, followed in female plants by strings of shiny red fruit. Hardy to 10°F (−12°C), US zones 8–10 or a little more. Native to the Himalayas and W China, where it grows in scrub and on forest margins.

Schisandra glaucescens   A deciduous climber that grows to 20ft (6m) with orange flowers in late spring or early summer, followed in female plants

Schisandra wild in the Lijiang Mountains, Yunnan

by strings of shiny red fruit. Hardy to 10°F (−12°C), US zones 8–10. Native to W China. The native American species, *Schisandra coccinea*, the Bay Star Vine or Wild Sasparilla, (*not illustrated*) is confined to the southeastern States. It has red flowers and spikes of fruit 1½in (4cm) long. Like magnolias, this is an example of similar plants which are found in eastern Asia and in the eastern States, but not in California or the northwest.

Actinidia kolomikta on a sunny wall at Kew

Schizophragma integrifolium on a shady wall

Decumaria barbara

Hydrangea

Climbing hydrangeas are a special group within this well-known genus. They are rather slow growing at first but well worth persisting with, as they are one of the only plants (apart from ivy) which will grow in the deep shade of a tree trunk.

PLANTING HELP   These will grow in any good soil and need a reasonable amount of water, especially in very dry summers. Excellent climbers for difficult positions on a shady wall or scrambling up the trunk of a full-grown tree.

Hydrangea serratifolia   An evergreen climber that grows to 17ft (5m) or more, with white flowers in a dense cluster in late summer. Native to Chile and Argentina. Hardy to 20°F (−6°C), US zones 9–10.

Hydrangea petiolaris   A deciduous shrub that can grow to 60ft (18m) or more in the wild, with large, flat clusters of numerous small, creamy white flowers that bloom in midsummer. Native to Japan, Korea and Taiwan. Hardy to −10°F (−23°C), US zones 6–9.

Schizophragma integrifolium   A very large, robust, deciduous climbing shrub that grows to 24ft (7m) tall, with long-lasting, showy clusters of white or pale pink flowers from summer to autumn. Native to central China. Hardy to −10°F (−23°C), US zones 6–9.

Decumaria

Decumaria barbara   A climbing semi-deciduous shrub that grows to 33ft (10m) tall, with clusters of creamy white flowers in early to midsummer. Native to eastern North America. Hardy to 10°F (−12°C), US zones 8–10 or perhaps a little lower.

PLANTING HELP   This plant makes small stem roots which allow it to climb up walls. Any soil in sun or part shade.

Kiwi Fruit or Chinese Gooseberry

Actinidia chinensis   A robust deciduous climber that grows to 26ft (8m) tall, with flowers opening creamy white, deepening with age, male and female on different plants, flowering in summer. Native to China. Hardy to 10°F (−12°C), US zones 8–10 or a little more.

CLIMBING HYDRANGEAS

Hydrangea petiolaris over an arch, with aquilegias and clipped box

Actinidia chinensis with male flowers

Hydrangea serratifolia

PLANTING HELP   Any soil, but best on a wall in sun or partial shade, although to get a good fruiting full sun and possibly some additional heat will be needed.

Actinidia kolomikta   A deciduous climbing shrub that grows to 30ft (9m) tall with leaves irregularly marked with pink or white and small, white fragrant flowers that appear in late spring or early summer. Native to China, Korea and Japan. Hardy to −20°F (−29°C), US zones 5–8.

PLANTING HELP   The coloured leaves develop best on mature plants in full sun on a wall. The root should be planted in the shade, with ample leaf mould in the soil.

Actinidia kolomikta

Clianthus puniceus 'Roseus' on a wall in Devon

Clianthus puniceus 'Albus'

Clianthus

Clianthus puniceus A spreading shrub that grows to 10ft (3m), with hanging bunches of large flowers, either red, pink **'Roseus'** or greenish white **'Albus'**, depending on the form, produced from winter to spring in gardens. Native to the coast of North Island, New Zealand. Hardy to 32°F (0°C), US zone 10 or a little lower. The various colour forms largely come true from seed.

PLANTING HELP   It will thrive in any good soil in a warm, sheltered position in frosty climates, protected from drying winds.

Ficus

Ficus pumila
An evergreen ivy-like climber that grows to 40ft (12m) tall and is powerful enough to cover a whole building. The leaves are very small when young but get larger as the plant matures. The figs

Ficus pumila 'Bellus'

Ficus pumila, juvenile form, creeping over a broken jar at Serre de la Madone, Menton

are large and blue. Native to Japan, China and Vietnam. Hardy to 20°F (–6°C), US zones 9–10.

***Ficus pumila* 'Bellus'** A variety with a white edge to the leaves.

PLANTING HELP One of the hardiest figs, this will sprout again if cut to the ground; it is best planted in the shade in sunny areas.

Mutisia

Mutisia decurrens
A suckering climber that grows to 10ft (3m) tall, with large vermilion, orange or deep yellow flowers in spring and summer. Native to Chile and Argentina. Hardy to 32°F (0°C), US zone 10.

PLANTING HELP
Easily grown in dry, sandy soil with the suckering rhizomes carefully protected.

Mutisia decurrens

Thunbergia alata

Black-eyed Susan

Thunbergia alata A small twining perennial plant with stems to 7ft (2m) long, and numerous funnel-shaped flowers, usually orange, but also yellow or white, with a distinctive very dark purple 'eye'. Native to tropical Africa but now also naturalized in many other countries, flowering in summer. Hardy to 32°F (0°C), US zone 10.

PLANTING HELP Good in a light, frost-free greenhouse or outside in mild areas. It is often grown as an annual in cooler climates.

Roses

Rosa is a large genus of around 150 species of deciduous or sometimes evergreen shrubs with erect, arching, scrambling or occasionally trailing stems with prickles or bristles, which originate in the temperate and subtropical zones of the Northern Hemisphere. There are also thousands of named cultivars and hybrids, as roses have been cultivated for thousands of years both in the Mediterranean area and in China. In ancient times roses were often cultivated for their oil which was used in cosmetics and in medicines.

The introduction of the perpetual-flowering China roses to Europe in the 18th century enabled breeders to produce varieties that bloomed from early summer to autumn, in a wide range of colours, so roses have become one of the most popular garden plants. The hybridization of roses over the last 200 years has made classification complex, but there are several main categories into which roses are usually divided. Our selection includes Wild roses, Old roses, Ramblers and Modern roses, the majority of which are well scented.

'Alister Stella Gray'

Old Roses

Climbing roses have always been popular, but it is difficult to raise climbers that flower more than once. The roses in this section are a selection of some of the very best of the older ones, most of which are summer-flowering only.

PLANTING & PRUNING HELP   Climbing roses will often grow and flower well with little pruning. To keep them tidy, or within bounds, prune off the shoots which have flowered and tie in the new shoots, either in late autumn or in early spring. Most roses will survive 0°F (−18°C), US zones 7–10, unless otherwise stated. Particularly hardy or tender ones have their temperatures and zones mentioned.

Rose 'Albéric Barbier'   A large-flowered Rambler that grows to 17ft (5m) with creamy yellow blooms that have one main flowering in the summer but continue to flower sporadically until autumn. Good scent. One of the best for summer-dry climates.

Rose 'Alister Stella Gray'   A Tea-Noisette that grows to 8ft (2.5m) as a shrub or 17ft (5m) if trained on a wall. The creamy yellow flowers appear in small clusters at the first flowering and then in large clusters on new shoots later in the year. Good scent.

Rose 'Blairii No. 2'   A China hybrid that can be trained as a climber, growing to 10ft (3m). It flowers mostly in summer with a few later blooms. Susceptible to mildew but a good scent.

Rose 'Blush Noisette'   The original Noisette rose makes a loose bush up to 8ft (2.5m) or grows to 17ft (5m) if trained on a wall. The small to medium flowers open pale pink from red-flushed buds and are produced in clusters continuously throughout the summer. It has good disease resistance and a sweet, clove-like scent.

Rose 'Mme Grégoire Staechelin'   A large-flowered climber that grows to 8ft (2.5m) or more. The pretty pink flowers are produced in early summer only and have a scent reminiscent of sweet peas.

'Blush Noisette'

'Mme Grégoire Staechelin'

'Blairii No. 2'

'Blush Noisette'

'Albéric Barbier' on an old wooden arbour

'Cécile Brünner'

little scent. Very attractive when allowed to scramble through a small tree.

Rose 'Céline Forestier' A Tea-Noisette climber that grows to 17ft (5m) in a warm situation. The pale yellow flowers are produced continuously and have a very good scent.

Rose 'Félicité et Perpétue' A semi-evergreen Rambler that can grow to 10ft (3m) or more. The creamy, pink-tinged flowers appear in late summer and have a delicate, primrose-like scent. Although liable to mildew, this rose is excellent for a cold, windy garden.

Rose 'Cécile Brünner' A small-flowered rose with Tea rose leaves that comes in two forms: a shrub form that grows to 3½ft (1m) high, raised in France by Veuve Ducher in 1881; and the climbing sport that grows to 20ft (6m) or more. It is repeat-flowering, although the pale pink blooms have

Rose 'Gloire de Dijon' A Tea-Bourbon hybrid, this all-time favourite climber grows to 13ft (4m) or more. The creamy yellow apricot flowers bloom in summer with some flowers produced into the autumn. In warm weather the pink tones become stronger and it has an excellent scent.

Rosa filipes 'Kiftsgate'

Rosa filipes 'Kiftsgate'   A small-flowered climber that grows to 40ft (12m). The single white flowers are produced profusely in huge heads in late summer. Well scented. This is one of the largest-growing roses that can be found, excellent to grow up a large tree or to cover an ugly shed or garage. Hardy to –10°F (–23°C), US zones 6–10.

Rose 'Sander's White Rambler'   A small-flowered, rampant rambler that grows to 13ft (4m). The small, white double blooms flower in late summer only and have quite a good scent. This rose will require some training and old wood should be removed each year after flowering. Hardy to –20°F (–29°C), US zones 5–10.

'Gloire de Dijon'

'Céline Forestier'

'Sander's White Rambler'

'Félicité et Perpétue'

'Chaplin's Pink Climber' and other Ramblers on a pergola at the Gardens of the Rose, St Albans

'François Juranville'

Rambling Roses

Ramblers normally throw up long non-flowering shoots each summer, which, in the second year, produce side shoots along their length bearing clusters of small flowers.

PRUNING HELP   Cut out the two-year-old stems which have flowered, so that the current year's long stems can be trained to flower for the next year.

Rose 'Alexandre Girault'   A massive Rambler that grows to at least 20ft (6m). The strong pink blooms appear in summer only. Good scent. Hardy to −10°F (−23°C), US zones 6–10.

Rose 'Chaplin's Pink Climber'   A very free-flowering Rambler that grows to 16ft (4.5m). The pink blooms are produced in large, dense clusters in the summer but have very little scent. Hardy to −20°F (−29°C), US zones 5–10.

'Alexandre Girault'

'Hiawatha'

Rose 'François Juranville' A large-flowered Rambler that grows to 24ft (7m) or more. The peach-coloured blooms are produced only in summer and have a good scent. Hardy to –10°F (–23°C), US zones 6–10.

'Veilchenblau'

Rose 'Léontine Gervais' A large-flowered Rambler that grows to 15ft (4.5m). The pale apricot flowers bloom only in the summer. Good scent. Hardy to –10°F (–23°C), US zones 6–10.

Rose 'Hiawatha' A vigorous free-growing Rambler that grows to 15ft (4.5m). The single, deep pink blooms with pale centres are produced in clusters and only in the summer. It is tolerant of shade and poor soils. Little scent. Hardy to –20°F (–29°C), US zones 5–10.

Rose 'Veilchenblau' A vigorous Rambler that grows to 24ft (7m). The small semi-double flowers of lavender purple are produced in large clusters and are only summer-flowering with a good scent. This is one of the bluest old roses. Hardy to –10°F (–23°C), US zones 6–10.

'Léontine Gervais'

'Alchymist' growing up an old apple tree

'Pink Perpétue'

'Handel'

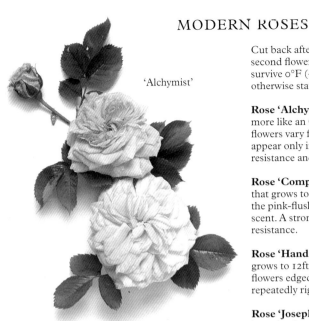

'Alchymist'

Cut back after the first flowering to encourage a second flowering later in the year. Most will survive 0°F (−18°C), US zones 7–10, unless otherwise stated.

Rose 'Alchymist' A modern climber that looks more like an Old rose and grows to 20ft (6m). The flowers vary from cream to apricot and peach and appear only in summer. It has good disease resistance and a fine scent.

Rose 'Compassion' A climbing Hybrid Tea that grows to 10ft (3m). It flowers repeatedly and the pink-flushed yellow blooms have an excellent scent. A strong, healthy grower with good disease resistance.

Rose 'Handel' A climbing Floribunda that grows to 12ft (3.5m). The very pretty pale pink flowers edged with darker pink produced repeatedly right through to winter. Slight scent.

Rose 'Joseph's Coat' A tall Floribunda that can be trained as a low climber and grows to 8ft (2.5m). The flowers, which open yellow and change to red and orange, appear right into winter but have little scent.

Modern Roses

Modern roses are complex crosses of Old roses crossed with the elegant Tea roses from China and with the repeat-flowering China roses, to give plants with a good second flowering.

PRUNING HELP   Modern roses should be carefully trained and weak and old wood removed.

Rose 'Morning Jewel' A climbing Floribunda that grows to 10ft (3m). The cerise pink flowers continue to bloom into the autumn and have a sweet scent.

Rose 'Pink Perpétue' A repeat-flowering Floribunda climber that grows to 10ft (3m). The pretty pink blooms have little scent.

'Compassion'

'Joseph's Coat' by a gingko in Eccleston Square

'Morning Jewel'

'New Dawn' growing on the wire fence of the tennis court in Eccleston Square

'Constance Spry' with wisteria

in midsummer, making a spectacular display and are very fragrant. It has good disease resistance and combines the health and vigour of Modern roses with the shape and scent of the Old roses.

Rose 'Danse des Sylphes'   A climbing repeat-flowering Floribunda that grows to 10ft (3m) or more. The crimson flowers have little scent.

'Eden Rose 88' (syn. 'Pierre de Ronsard') A superb low climber or large shrub rose that grows to 8ft (2.5m). The pale pink blooms with a greenish tinge appear throughout summer and have some scent.

'Eden Rose 88'

Rose 'Albertine'   A stiff, large-flowered Rambler that grows to 20ft (6m). The pale pink flowers are produced in one spectacular display in summer and are very well scented. Most suitable for training along a hedge or low wall.

Rose 'Maigold'   A large-flowered climber that grows to 20ft (6m). The yellow blooms are produced only in spring and have some scent.

Rose 'New Dawn'   A repeat-flowering sport of the Rambler 'Dr W. Van Fleet', that grows to 20ft (6m). The pale pink blooms have some scent. This is one of the most satisfactory and long-flowering climbers in English and American gardens.

Rose 'Constance Spry'   David Austin's first English rose is a large shrub or climber that grows to 13ft (4m) if trained as a climber and 7ft (2m) tall and wide if grown as a shrub. The big, beautifully shaped pink flowers bloom only once,

Rose 'Paul's Lemon Pillar' A climbing Hybrid Tea that grows to 20ft (6m). The pale yellow flowers appear only in summer and are strongly scented.

'Paul's Lemon Pillar'

'Albertine'

'Danse des Sylphes' at Kew

'Maigold' with a golden *Cornus*

Passiflora mollissima on a tree in Mexico

Passion Flowers

There are about 450 species of Passion flower; most are vines, but a few are shrubs, erect herbs or small trees. They originate from the tropical Americas, Asia, Australia and Polynesia. Most species have excellent edible fruits.

PLANTING & PRUNING HELP   Passion flowers need well-drained soil to thrive as their roots are liable to rot if they become water-logged. Avoid a peat-based compost and choose one with a mixture of sand, gravel, coarse peat and loam. Many species can stand a short period of frost but if prolonged frozen conditions are expected, it is worth using an electric heating cable near the roots. Passion flowers will do well if fed regularly with a high potash liquid fertilizer during the growing season, and while growing well they still need frequent feeding. Once established, prune annually to get rid of dead growth in the centre and cut unwanted branches back to the base.

Passiflora mollissima

Passiflora alata   A rampant woody climber that grows to 30ft (10m) or more with fragrant, dark brownish red flowers through the year but mainly in summer in cultivation. Fruit edible, orange or red when ripe. Hardy to 20°F (–6°C), US zones 9–10. Native to Brazil.

Passiflora antioquiensis   A slender woody climber that grows to 17ft (5m) with solitary, pendent, pinkish red flowers mainly in the summer in cultivation. Fruit edible, like a small banana, yellow when ripe. Hardy to 32°F (0°C), US zone 10 or a little more, for short periods. Native to Colombia.

Passiflora mollissima   A rampant climber that grows to 30ft (10m) or more, with pale pink flowers from summer to autumn in cultivation. Fruit edible, like a small banana, yellow and downy when ripe. Hardy to 20°F (–6°C), US zones 9–10. Native to W Venezuela, Colombia, SE Peru, and W Bolivia.

Passiflora vitifolia (syn. *Passiflora sanguinea*) A vigorous woody climber that grows to 50ft (15m) with bright scarlet upright flowers from summer to autumn in cultivation. Fruit edible, dark green mottled with white. Hardy to 32°F (0°C), US zone 10. Native to Nicaragua, Costa Rica, Colombia, Ecuador and Peru.

Passiflora vitifolia

Passiflora antioquiensis

Passiflora alata

Passiflora vitifolia

Passiflora mollissima

Specimens from the National Collection at Kingston Seymour, Somerset, ⅓ life-size

Passiflora caerulea in the conservatory at Syon House, west London

Passiflora 'Incense'   *Passiflora quadrangularis*   *P. caerulea* 'Constance Elliot'

Passiflora racemosa in a warm greenhouse at the
Royal Botanic Garden, Edinburgh

Passiflora racemosa

Passiflora caerulea   A vigorous climber that grows to 30ft (10m) or more with solitary, slightly fragrant flowers, white with purple filaments, mainly in summer in cultivation. Fruit edible, but rather insipid, bright orange with red seeds when ripe. Hardy to −10°F (−23°C), US zones 6–9. Native to South America from east-central Brazil to Argentina.

Passiflora caerulea 'Constance Elliot'
This variety has fragrant, creamy white flowers and will survive outside in mild areas if given the protection of a wall but is best kept frost-free.

Passiflora 'Incense'   A new American cultivar which grows very vigorously and blooms profusely with fragrant, deep purple flowers produced throughout summer and autumn. Fruit edible, light olive green when ripe. Not easy to grow in cool-summer areas, though hardy to 20°F (−6°C), US zones 9–10 or a little more for short periods.

Passiflora quadrangularis
A huge woody climber that grows to 50ft (15m) or more with dark crimson flowers that bloom mainly in summer in cultivation. Fruit edible, the largest of any passion flower, greenish orange when ripe. Hardy

to 32°F (0°C), US zone 10. Native to Central America and the West Indies and now found throughout the tropics.

Passiflora racemosa   An evergreen vine that grows to 30ft (10m) in warm countries but only 17ft (5m) under glass. Hanging racemes of red flowers bloom most of the summer and autumn. Fruit edible, but rather insipid; bright orange with red seeds when ripe. Hardy to 32°F (0°C), US zone 10. Native to Brazil.

Passiflora caerulea

71

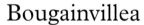

Bougainvillea with *Lantana* in Mexico

Bougainvillea 'Golden Glow'

'Mary Palmer' and 'Mary Palmer's Enchantment'

Bougainvillea

Bougainvillea belongs to the family *Nyctaginaceae* and is a small genus of about 18 species of deciduous, shrubby, climbing or creeping plants and small trees. They come from tropical South and Central America and numerous beautiful hybrids, cultivars and mutations have been developed.

PLANTING & PRUNING HELP   In their natural habitat bougainvilleas scramble up into trees and other shrubs. In cooler climates they make excellent conservatory plants when grown in pots in a mixture of loam and peat-based compost but they need plenty of light, adequate water and regular feeding with a high nitrogen fertilizer during the growing season. Provide a trellis or wires for them to climb up. During cold weather reduce watering to a minimum; the plant will often drop its leaves and become semi-dormant. After the winter rest remove dead shoots and straggly stems and cut the side shoots well back to encourage new growth in the spring.

Bougainvillea glabra   A vigorous climbing shrub that grows to 25ft (8m) outside but only about 8ft (2.5m) in a pot. Showy, reddish purple bracts surround insignificant white flowers which bloom almost continuously in their native habitat. Hardy to 20°F (−6°C), US zones 9–10 or cooler for short periods once the plants have become established. Native to Brazil.

'Alison Davey'   A free-flowering, medium- to large-sized plant. The showy, rounded bracts open orange red, becoming deep magenta later. The creamy white flowers are conspicuous.
'Brazilian'   A variety with purple bracts surrounding conspicuous cream-coloured flowers.
'Daphne Mason'   A free-flowering, moderately vigorous sport with showy bracts that open orange pink and change to violet purple, and creamy white flowers that are quite large and conspicuous.
'Jennifer Fernie'   A moderately vigorous cultivar of *Bougainvillea glabra* with beautiful, pure white bracts.
'Mary Palmer'   A bicoloured bud sport in which some of the bracts are soft pink becoming white while others are purple.
'Mary Palmer's Enchantment'   A white-bracted sport of *Bougainvillea* 'Mary Palmer'.
'Ralph Sander'   A very attractive, white-bracted cultivar with green veining.
'Golden Glow'   A very free-flowering cultivar with golden orange yellow bracts.

Bougainvillea forming a hedge in Nairobi   *Bougainvillea* climbing on a trellis

Top row (left to right) 'Daphne Mason', 'Alison Davey', 'Jennifer Fernie', 'Brazilian'; bottom row 'Mary Palmer's Enchantment', 'Mary Palmer' and 'Ralph Sander'; photographed in Nairobi

Wild morning glory *Ipomoea tricolor* climbing over bushes in central Mexico, south of Lake Chapala

Morning Glory

Morning glory, *Ipomoea*, belongs to the family *Convolvulaceae* and is a large and variable genus of 450–500 species of annual and perennial herbs, shrubs and small trees. It is widely distributed in tropical and subtropical regions and many herbaceous species, which are perennial in their native habitat, can be grown as annuals in areas with hot, moist summers and cold winters. Several species of morning glory have important economic uses, the principal one being *Ipomoea batatas* which is the sweet potato, a staple in the diet of people living in the tropics, especially in Central America. Other species are important in traditional medicine or as soil-binders in dry arid regions. Where climate permits, many species are grown for the ornamental value of their showy flowers.

PLANTING HELP   In warm climates grow morning glory in well-drained, sandy loam; in cool, temperate areas grow under glass in pots and tubs in fertile, loam-based soil, in medium to high humidity, watering abundantly during the growing season. Vigorous hardy species can be grown in borders of fertile, well-drained loam in a warm, sunny site and treated as frost-tender annuals. Prune perennials in late winter or spring to thin out old tangled growth.

Ipomoea lobata (syn. *Mina lobata*)   An annual or short-lived perennial that grows to 17ft (5m) tall with small flowers that are red before they open, fading to yellow and then becoming white. Hardy to 32°F (0°C), US zone 10. Native to Mexico.

Ipomoea purpurea   An annual or short-lived perennial that grows to 17ft (5m) tall and bears deep blue or purple flowers in summer. Hardy to 32°F (0°C), US zone 10. Thought to be native to Mexico but widely grown and naturalized elsewhere.

Moonflower *Ipomoea alba*   A perennial climber, woody at the base, that grows to 100ft (30m) tall and in summer produces beautiful, large, white flowers tinged with green on the outside, that are fragrant at night. Hardy to 32°F (0°C), US zone 10. Native throughout the tropics.

Ipomoea tricolor **'Heavenly Blue'**   A climbing annual or perennial that grows to 12ft (3.5m) tall and bears lovely pale blue flowers in the summer. Hardy to 32°F (0°C), US zone 10. Native to Mexico and Central America. This is a beautiful climber for a sunny wall or a conservatory. It is very susceptible to red spider when grown under glass or in a dry site, and needs humidity while growing, but will tolerate and even prefers much drier conditions while it is in flower.

MORNING GLORY

Moonflower *Ipomoea alba* in the south of France

Ipomoea tricolor 'Heavenly Blue'

Ipomoea purpurea, a perennial with deep blue flowers, becoming purple as they fade

Ipomoea lobata with red buds and white flowers with protruding stamens, climbing on a fence

Solanum crispum 'Glasnevin' at Gravetye Manor, Sussex

Solanum jasminoides 'Album'

Plumbago auriculata

Plumbago

Plumbago auriculata (syn. *Plumbago capensis*)
A scrambling or loose-growing climbing shrub
with masses of lovely pale blue flowers, reaching
6ft (1.8m) or more if supported. Native to South
Africa. Tolerant of heat and drought, and will
stand some frost overnight.

PLANTING HELP   Plumbago is a good plant
for a hedge in mild areas, or in colder parts it is a
superb trouble-free plant for the greenhouse. It is
fast growing and very free flowering. Should it be
damaged by frost it will almost certainly come
again from the base. Hardy to 20°F (–6°C),
US zones 9–10.

Potato Vines

Solanum is a very large genus of about 1400
species of herbs, shrubs, trees and occasionally
vines. They have a cosmopolitan distribution and
are found particularly in tropical America. This
huge genus includes weeds, plants that are grown
for food, such as potatoes, and many ornamental
shrubs, climbers and perennials.

Solanum wendlandii

PLANTING HELP   The climbing species
mentioned here can either be grown up pergolas
and trelliswork in warm temperate regions or they
can be grown in a greenhouse or conservatory in
cooler areas. They all like warm south or
southwest-facing walls and thrive in full sun and
most kinds of soil, a medium fertility, loam-based
mix being best. Water well and prune immediately
after flowering or in spring before growth begins.

Solanum crispum 'Glasnevin'   A vigorous
shrub climbing to 13ft (4m) with large clusters of
fragrant, mauve blue flowers with golden yellow
stamens in summer. Hardy to 10°F (–12°C), US
zones 8–10. Native to Chile.

Solanum seaforthianum at the Plantsman Nursery,
Throwleigh, Devon

Solanum jasminoides 'Album'
A deciduous shrubby climber that grows
to 20ft (6m) with pure
white, star-shaped
flowers, opening from
pale mauve buds
over a long
period in
summer and
autumn. Hardy
to 32°F (0°C),
US zone 10.
Native to Brazil.

Solanum crispum
'Glasnevin'

Solanum seaforthianum   A slender, hairless,
scrambling evergreen shrub that grows to 20ft
(6m) with hanging clusters of starry, light violet
blue flowers appearing in summer. Hardy to 32°F
(0°C), US zone 10. Native to Trinidad and South
America. The starry flowers and divided leaves
give this species the appearance of a jasmine.

Solanum wendlandii Paradise Flower
A vigorous, scrambling, more or less evergreen
hairless climber with spiny branches that grows to
17ft (5m), with huge, branched clusters of large
rounded, lilac blue flowers throughout the
summer. Hardy to 32°F (0°C), US zone 10.
Native to Costa Rica.

Lapageria rosea
'Nash Court'

Lapageria

Lapageria rosea An evergreen climber with stiff leathery leaves and wiry stems twining to 10ft (3m) or more. The large waxy bells of red, pink or white, appear mainly from late summer to spring. Hardy to 20°F (–6°C), US zones 9–10. Native to Chile, where it is the national flower, and southern Argentina, growing in wet forests. Named after the Empress Josephine, whose maiden name was de la Pagerie.

PLANTING HELP Prefers a moist leafy soil and shelter; an ideal plant for a cold and shaded conservatory, needing little care except protection of the young shoots from slugs and snails. Slow to establish, but very long-lived.

Sollya

Lapageria rosea 'Nash Court'

Sollya heterophylla A delicate climber or twiggy shrub with stems that grows to 7ft (2m). The blue, bell-like flowers appear from late summer through to late autumn. Hardy to 32°F (0°C), US zone 10. Native to Western Australia.

PLANTING HELP Needs moist soil with good drainage. Best grown in full sun on a sheltered wall or in a light conservatory.

Rhodochiton

Rhodochiton atrosanguineus (syn. *R. volubilis*) A delicate climber that grows to 7ft (2m) or more by scrambling over shrubs and small trees, with stems climbing by twisting leaf stalks. The hanging flowers have a wide, reddish cup of sepals on the outside and a blackish purple tubular corolla inside and appear mainly in late summer and autumn. Hardy to 32°F (0°C), US zone 10. Native to SW Mexico, growing in moist forest.

PLANTING HELP Although perennial, this climber can be grown as an annual, planted early indoors and grown in warm humid conditions until summer, when it will continue flowering up to the first frost in a shady place outside.

Rhodochiton atrosanguineus

Sollya heterophylla

Canarina canariensis

Canarina canariensis wild in heather forest

Canarina

Canarina canariensis
A clambering perennial with a large fleshy root and annual succulent stems that grows to 10ft (3m). The bell-like flowers are orange to red with darker veins and copious watery nectar, and appear from autumn through the winter to spring. Hardy to 32°F (0°C), US zone 10. Native to the Canary Islands, where it grows in tree heather forests and among brambles.

PLANTING HELP   Easily grown in a frost-free greenhouse in sandy leafy soil, and kept dry in summer. Growth starts in August and flowering will continue through the winter if the plant has enough warmth and light. The leaves will survive a light frost.

Canarina canariensis wild on Tenerife

Campsis grandiflora with Agapanthus at La Mortola

Campsis grandiflora in central Italy

Campsis radicans in Kent

Bignonia

The genus *Campsis*, commonly called Bignonia, consists of only two species known as Trumpet Vines. They are fast-growing deciduous climbers that cling by aerial roots.

PLANTING HELP   *Campsis* are fast growing and may flower better in a rather poor soil; they need full sun and added heat from a wall for optimum flowering. Prune back some of last year's growth in the spring to get better flowering.

Campsis grandiflora   A deciduous climber that grows to 20ft (6m) or more with large, wide-mouthed apricot orange flowers in mid- and late summer. Hardy to 10°F (–12°C), US zones 8–10. Native to China.

Campsis radicans   A woody climber that grows to 70ft (20m) with large, tubular orange red flowers in mid- and late summer. Hardy to 0°F (–18°C), US zones 7–10. Native to North America. This species is freer flowering in cool climates than *Campsis grandiflora*.

Distictis buccinatoria

Distictis buccinatoria at La Mortola

Mandevilla suaveolens at Ventnor, Isle of Wight

Distictis

Distictis buccinatoria (syn. *Phaedranthus buccinatorius*)   A rampant climber that grows to 35ft (10m) or more with large, tubular, bright red flowers with an orange tube in summer. Hardy to 32°F (0°C), US zone 10 or a little more. Native to Mexico.

PLANTING HELP   Best on a sunny wall in borderline areas and good in the warmest gardens along the Mediterranean coastline, in Florida, California and Australia.

Mandevilla

Mandevilla suaveolens   A large twining climber that grows to 17ft (5m) with clusters of large creamy white, fragrant flowers from early to late summer. Hardy to 20°F (–6°C), US zones 9–10. Native to Argentina.

PLANTING HELP   Thrives in any fertile soil but needs full sun and the heat from a sunny wall to flower well.

81

Antigonum

Antigonum leptopus A rampant tropical climber with tuberous roots and stems that grow to 40ft (12m) tall, with bright crimson pink flowers in summer and autumn. Native to the coastal plains of Mexico. Hardy to 32°F (0°C), US zone 10.

PLANTING HELP This requires a hot position with ample water in summer; good in desert climates where it may go dormant if dry in summer, or continue growing if well watered.

Russian Vine

Polygonum baldschuanicum A very large, twining deciduous climber that grows to 24ft (7m) tall, with large clusters of tiny, scented, creamy pink flowers that appear in late summer to autumn. Native to central Asia. Hardy to −20°F (−29°C), US zones 5–9.

PLANTING HELP Excellent for covering ugly sheds but it can easily get out of control if not pruned back after flowering. Thrives in any good soil.

Tweedia caerulea

Cruel Plant *Araujia sericofera*

Antigonum leptopus in Bermuda

Golden Hop *Humulus lupulus*

Cruel Plant

Araujia sericofera   A twining woody
subtropical climber that grows to 30ft (10m) tall,
with scented, whitish flowers in late summer;
these trap moths by their tongues, hence the
common name. Native to Brazil and Peru, and
naturalized in northern Australia. Hardy to 32°F
(0°C), US zone 10.

Russian Vine *Polygonum baldschuanicum* at Tapeley
Park near Bideford, Devon

PLANTING HELP   Easily grown in any frost-
free area or in a conservatory with sufficient heat
to keep out the frost.

Tweedia

Tweedia caerulea (syn. *Oxypetalum caeruleum*)
A woody climber that grows to 4ft (1.2m) tall, with
clusters of flowers that are pale azure blue when
they open in summer, then becoming purplish
with age and finally fading to lilac. Native to Chile.
Hardy to 20°F (–6°C), US zones 9–10.

PLANTING HELP   Thrives in any fertile soil
but requires a warm sheltered spot in cool climates.

Golden Hop

Humulus lupulus '**Aureus**'   A yellow-leaved
variety of the common hop, which is a twining
herbaceous perennial with stems that grow to 20ft
(6m) tall. The straw-coloured male flowers open in
late June; the females develop into hops in August;
the golden hop is female, but seldom fruits. Native
to Europe and western and central Asia. Hardy to
0°F (–18°C), US zones 7–10.

PLANTING HELP   Grows in any soil,
preferably in a warm, sheltered position. A useful
plant to cover an unsightly shed or fence, drought-
resistant once established.

Garden Nasturtium *Tropaeolum majus*

Canary Creeper *Tropaeolum peregrinum*

Nasturtiums

Nasturtiums or *Tropaeolum* belong to the family *Tropaeolaceae*. The genus *Tropaeolum* contains about 86 species of annuals and herbaceous perennials, sometimes with tuberous roots, either vine-like or compact and bushy. Nasturtiums come from southern Mexico, south to Chile and Patagonia and there are numerous cultivars, particularly of the annual *Tropaeolum majus*. Generally they are grown in gardens for their colour and ornamental value, the dwarf varieties either as edging plants or in borders and the semi-trailing types for hanging baskets or up fences or other supports.

PLANTING HELP Annuals and perennials will thrive in well-drained, moisture-retentive soil with low fertility in a sunny position but the perennials are hardier and will even tolerate a certain amount of cold. *Tropaeolum tuberosum* can even survive a short, light frost if it is grown in a warm, sheltered position with good drainage. *T. speciosum* thrives best where there are cool, moist summers, such as in north and west Britain, yet it is also tolerant of chalk.

Flame Nasturtium *Tropaeolum speciosum*
A tall perennial climber with a fleshy rhizome. Stems grow to 10ft (3m) with bright red flowers in summer, followed by bluish fruit. Hardy to 10°F (−12°C), US zones 8–10. Native to Chile. Good grown on walls or on holly or yew hedges; if not supported, it makes a useful ground-cover.

Tropaeolum tuberosum A tall climber with tuberous roots and stems that climb to 10ft (3m) or more. The flowers have deep yellow petals with red sepals and bloom in autumn. Hardy to 10°F (−12°C), US zones 8–10. Native to Peru, Bolivia, Colombia and Ecuador. In the high Andes the knobbly tubers, which are yellow streaked red, are grown as a vegetable. The variety **'Ken Aslet'** has the advantage of flowering from midsummer onwards as it is not affected by day length. Most clones do not begin to form buds until the long nights of autumn. In frosty climates this plant can be treated like a potato and lifted in autumn, kept indoors and planted out again when the danger of hard frost has passed.

Tropaeolum ciliatum A delicate but rampant climber spreading from thin white roots and with stems that grow to 10ft (3m) with yellow flowers that bloom in the summer. Hardy to 32°F (0°C), US zone 10 or a little more if the roots are protected.

Garden Nasturtium *Tropaeolum majus*
These exotic annuals grow to 6ft (1.8m) tall and produce yellow, orange or red flowers, single or double, in the summer. There are many garden varieties; they can be made to climb, but most are ground-covering scramblers which look best spreading across gravel areas. There are also several compact non-trailing varieties. Hardy to 10°F (−12°C), US zones 8–10. Native to South America.

Canary Creeper *Tropaeolum peregrinum*
A half-hardy annual or perennial climber that grows to 8ft (2.5m) tall with smallish lemon to sulphur yellow flowers that bloom from summer to autumn. Hardy to 20°F (−6°C), US zones 9–10. Native to Peru and Ecuador.

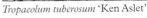

Tropaeolum tuberosum 'Ken Aslet' in Eccleston Square

Tropaeolum tuberosum 'Ken Aslet'

Tropaeolum ciliatum

Tropaeolum speciosum growing over a yew hedge

Climbing Dicentra *Dicentra likiangensis* climbing over a holly tree in Devon

Eccremocarpus

Eccremocarpus scaber A perennial tendril-climber that scrambles up to 10ft (3m), with scarlet, orange or yellow flowers from summer to autumn, followed by swollen seed pods full of thin, dry seeds. Hardy to 20°F (−6°C), US zones 9–10. Native to Chile.

PLANTING HELP   Grow in well-drained, fertile soil. It will tolerate partial shade but flowers more profusely in full sun. Can also be grown in a tub in a cool conservatory.

Climbing Dicentra

Dicentra likiangensis   An herbaceous climber with umbels of yellow hanging flowers and red fleshy fruit. Stems annual, climbing to 10ft (3m), from a perennial rootstock. Flowers ¾in (2cm) long; the red fleshy fruits are 1¼in (3cm) long, cylindrical. In the related *Dicentra scandens*, (*not illustrated*) the flowers are smaller, the fruits flat and green. Hardy to

10°F (−12°C), US zones 8–10 or a little more. Native to SW China and Bhutan.

PLANTING HELP   This unusual plant has very delicate open growth and prefers good soil. The roots can be planted in the shade, allowing the plant to scramble up through a shrub into the sunlight or it can be trained to grow on a wall.

Climbing Dicentra

Holboellia coriacea

Stauntonia

Stauntonia hexaphylla A large evergreen climber that grows to 33ft (10m) with attractive leaves that have 3–7 stalked, hanging leaflets and umbels of pale greyish mauve, scented flowers, the male and female on different plants. Native to Japan, Korea and Taiwan. Hardy to 20°F (–6°C), US zones 9–10.

PLANTING HELP Stauntonia will grow in any moderately good soil, scrambling up through a large tree or trained on a wall in mild areas. It prefers full sun.

Holboellia

A small genus of five species from India, the Himalayas and China. They are evergreen climbing shrubs with flowers growing in separate inflorescences.

PLANTING HELP Easily cultivated on a sheltered wall. Any soil; sun or shade with moist leafy soil at the root.

Holboellia latifolia A large evergreen twining shrub that grows to 17ft (5m) with fragrant male and female flowers in separate inflorescences, the male green white, the female purple, blooming in spring. Edible purplish fruit are formed in warm summers. Hardy to 20°F (–6°C), US zones 9–10. Native to the Himalayas.

Holboellia coriacea An evergreen climber that grows to 17ft (5m) with fragrant male and female flowers in separate inflorescences, the male white, the female purplish, blooming in early summer. Hardy to 10°F (–12°C), US zones 8–10 or a little more. Native to China.

Eccremocarpus scaber

Holboellia latifolia

Stauntonia hexaphylla at Cannington, Somerset

Virginia Creeper *Parthenocissus quinquefolia*   Boston Ivy *Parthenocissus tricuspidata*

Boston Ivy *Parthenocissus tricuspidata* in autumn colour

Virginia Creeper

Virginia Creeper belongs to a small genus of 10 species of generally deciduous, trailing or ascending woody vines. They are native to North America, east Asia and the Himalayas. Virginia Creeper is characterized by its tendrils or adhesive pads by which it clambers upwards towards the light. There are a number of cultivars and many of the most commonly cultivated species have escaped from gardens and become naturalized in the wild. Virginia Creeper species are grown for their foliage and are particularly striking in autumn when the leaves display a wonderful range of scarlet and crimson. They are commonly grown to cover up unsightly walls and are excellent for climbing up trees, fences, pergolas and buildings. It is also possible to grow them in pots.

PLANTING HELP   Virginia Creepers prefer moist soils and need at least some sun to ensure good autumn colour. *Parthenocissus quinquefolia* is quite hardy and should be grown on an east- or west-facing wall in partial shade. *Parthenocissus tricuspidata* is not quite as hardy and can be grown in a position of partial shade or on a sun-free wall. Both are vigorous climbers and should be pruned back annually, in autumn or early winter, to prevent growth reaching under house eaves and tiles.

Virginia Creeper *Parthenocissus quinquefolia*
A vigorous deciduous climber that grows to 60ft (18m) tall and capable of a similar spread. The stems cling to the wall by adhesive-tipped tendrils, and the leaves, with 3–7 separate leaflets, turn to brilliant orange and crimson before falling. Hardy to –10°F (–23°C), US zones 6–9 or lower. Native to eastern North America.

Boston Ivy *Parthenocissus tricuspidata*
A deciduous climber that grows to 60ft (18m) tall and wide where space is available, with tiny, inconspicuous greenish flowers. The stems cling to the wall by adhesive-tipped tendrils, and the leaves, with 3–5 lobes, turn bright crimson before falling. Hardy to at least 10°F (–12°C), US zones 8–10, possibly more. Native to Japan, Korea and China.

Celastrus

Often called Bittersweet in America, *Celastrus* belongs to the Spindleberry family; it should not be confused with English Bittersweet or Woody Nightshade *Solanum dulcamara*. *Celastrus* is a genus of some 30 species of shrubs, usually deciduous and very occasionally evergreen, generally climbing or twining. They are native to Africa, America, Australia, east and south Asia and the Pacific. These rampant, vigorous climbers are easily cultivated and excellent for growing over old stumps or through sturdy living trees.

PLANTING HELP   Bittersweet species are happy either in full sun or partial shade and are perfectly hardy. Although they can be propagated from seed, this method is unreliable because this genus has male and female flowers on different plants and the sex of the plant cannot be determined until they reach maturity. Propagation by root cuttings taken from female plants in late winter is easier and these cuttings should be placed in a cold frame in equal parts of sand and peat.

Oriental Bittersweet
Celastrus orbiculatus
A densely climbing shrub that grows to 40ft (12m) tall with tiny, pale green flowers in early to midsummer and long, pale green leaves. The fruits are coral pink to red, from a splitting orange husk and in good forms appear prolifically in bead-like bunches in autumn. Hardy to –10°F (–23°C), US zones 6–9 or lower. Native to Japan, China, Korea and naturalized in North America.

Oriental
Bittersweet
*Celastrus
orbiculatus*

Boston Ivy *Parthenocissus tricuspidata* in fruit

Grape vines with ground-cover of Golden Marjoram at Powis Castle

Vitis vinifera 'Brant' at the Savill Garden

Grape Vines

Grape vines belong to the family *Vitaceae*; there are about 65 species in the genus *Vitis*, mainly sprawling vines or shrubs. They are native to the Northern Hemisphere, particularly Asia and North America; some species are grown for the value of their fruit, while others are grown for ornament, for their luxuriant autumn foliage which grows up pergolas, walls, fences, walkways and through trees. Vines have been cultivated for many centuries which has caused some confusion in the naming of varieties in Europe and the Middle East.

PLANTING HELP   Vines should be grown in deep, moist, well-drained, preferably chalky soil. The species mentioned here will all thrive in sun or part shade but ideally need a warm situation if

Vitis vinifera 'Incana' in autumn

Vitis vinifera 'Purpurea'

they are to produce ripe fruit and good autumn colours. Prune in mid-winter and if growing on a support system, make sure that it is strong enough and high enough to sustain the weight of the foliage which can grow as much as 7ft (2m) in a season.

Vitis coignetiae in early autumn

Vitis coignetiae A deciduous vine climbing high into forest trees up to 85ft (25m) with huge, wrinkled, veiny leaves that turn purplish or red in autumn. The small black fruits grow in long, narrow branches and are scarcely edible. Hardy to −10°F (−23°C), US zones 6–9 or a little more. Native to Japan and Korea.

Common Grape Vine *Vitis vinifera* A high-climbing vine with stems up to 120ft (35m) in the wild but generally 3½ft–10ft (1–3m) in cultivation by annual pruning. It has large lobed leaves and numerous small, pale green flowers that bloom in late spring or early summer. The variable coloured grapes ripen in late summer. Hardy to 0°F (−18°C), US zones 7–10. Native to southern and central Europe.

Vitis vinifera 'Brant' This hybrid has small, sweet black grapes and leaves which turn red with contrasting green veins, in late summer.

Vitis vinifera 'Incana' This variety has leaves covered in fine white hairs, especially when young, and black grapes. The autumn leaves turn various shades of pale red.

Vitis vinifera 'Purpurea' This variety has leaves which are rich reddish purple with a bloom when young, later dark purplish with small black grapes.

Vitis coignetiae in summer on a pillar

Cotoneaster
'Cornubia'

Cotoneaster

A large genus of shrubs and trees from Europe, Asia and North Africa; although they have attractive white flowers in spring, they are grown mainly for their display of attractive berries in autumn and winter.

Cotoneaster horizontalis

PLANTING HELP
Cotoneasters thrive in any soil including chalky soil. They can be grown as free-standing bushes but will look their best when trained on a sunny wall.

Cotoneaster bullatus   A deciduous shrub or small tree that can grow to 26ft (8m) tall but usually grows to about 10ft (3m). The small pink flowers appear in early to midsummer and the bright red berries fruit in autumn. Native to China. Hardy to 0°F (−18°C), US zones 7–10 or a little colder.

Cotoneaster cochleatus   An evergreen shrub that grows to 1ft (30cm) tall but spreads to a width of up to 6ft (1.8m). The tiny flowers appear in early summer and the bright red berries appear in autumn. Hardy to −10°F (−23°C), US zones 6–9.

Cotoneaster cochleatus cascading over rocks

Cotoneaster '**Cornubia**'   A variety that makes a large spreading shrub with arching branches, growing to 24ft (7m) high and as much across, with bright red berries that appear in late summer. Hardy to −10°F (−23°C), US zones 6–9.

Cotoneaster horizontalis   A deciduous sprawling shrub with attractive horizontal branches, growing to 7ft (2m) across, with pinkish flowers in midsummer (much loved by queen wasps), and bright red berries that fruit in late autumn. Native to China. Hardy to −10°F (−23°C), US zones 6–9 or a little colder.

Cotoneaster salicifolius   An evergreen or semi-evergreen shrub with arching branches that grows to 13ft (4m) tall, with bright red berries that fruit in late autumn to early winter. Native to China. Hardy to 0°F (−18°C), US zones 7–10 or a little colder.

Pyracantha 'Orange Glow' on the wall of a Dorset cottage

Pyracantha

A small genus of 7 thorny shrubs from SE Europe right across to China; although they have attractive white flowers in spring they are grown mainly for their very showy display of attractive berries in autumn and winter. Pyracanthus make very useful hedging plants as their thorny stems keep out all intruders.

PLANTING HELP   Pyracanthas fruit best in a sheltered site by a sunny wall where the brightly coloured masses of berries can be enjoyed from autumn to winter.

Pyracantha atalantoides   An evergreen shrub that grows to 20ft (6m) tall, with tiny white flowers that bloom in summer and orange red berries that fruit throughout the winter. Native to China. Hardy to 10°F (–12°C), US zones 8–10 or a little colder.

Pyracantha atalantoides

Pyracantha 'Orange Glow'   An evergreen shrub that grows up to 17ft (5m) tall and often wider, with clusters of white hawthorn-like flowers that appear in spring and bright reddish orange berries that fruit well into the winter if not eaten by birds. Hardy to 0°F (–18°C), US zones 7–10.

Pyracantha 'Soleil d'Or'   This hybrid is a low-growing shrub with yellow orange berries.

Pyracantha 'Soleil d'Or'

Cotoneaster bullatus

Cotoneaster salicifolius

Cotoneaster cochleatus on the rock garden at Kew

Index

INDEX